Basil Woodd

The Psalms of David

And other Portions of the Sacred Scriptures

Basil Woodd

The Psalms of David
And other Portions of the Sacred Scriptures

ISBN/EAN: 9783337341015

Printed in Europe, USA, Canada, Australia, Japan

Cover: Foto ©Lupo / pixelio.de

More available books at **www.hansebooks.com**

It is

LONDON:
Printed and Sold by WATTS and
No. 31, South-Molton Street, O

Price 5s. in common Binding.

PREFACE.

IT has frequently been observed that PRAISE is the noblest employ of the Church of God, and that it bears the nearest affinity to the employ of heaven.—To this subject the inspired Psalmist tuned his lyre, and observed that *whoso offereth praise, glorifieth God*—Psalm 1. In singing the praises of God, Paul and Silas found their happiness in a dungeon—Acts xvi. 25. The incarnate Saviour composed his mind in the immediate prospect of his agony, by *singing an hymn with his disciples*—Matt. xxvi. 30.

The divine authority thus sanctions and commands the holy employ, *Let the word of Christ dwell in you richly in all wisdom; teaching and admonishing one another in psalms, and hymns, and spiritual songs, singing with grace in your hearts to the Lord*—Col. iii. 116.

To assist the pious worshipper in this most divine service, is the object of the following Collection of Psalms and Hymns.

The selection principally is compiled from versions of the Psalms of David, or select portions of the Psalms, and of Holy Scripture.

To obviate the prejudices which have been too generally adopted against all compositions of this nature, excepting the Old and New Versions of the Psalms,—it has been judged expedient just to observe, that it does not appear that the old version of Sternhold and Hopkins ever received the Royal Sanction, though by degrees the version was introduced in all Parochial Churches.—Vide Heylin's Church History, p 25.

The version of Tate and Brady received the allowance of the King in council, and the recommendation of the Bishop of London: but neither version was ever *enjoined* to be used in Churches.

It rather seems evident from the Statutes and Acts, which have any reference to this subject, that an indulgence is granted to every other version, and even to all Prayers and Selections, provided they are really translated from the inspired Writings. The clauses of the Acts referred to, are here subjoined.

The Statute of the 2nd and 3rd of Edw. VI. ch. i. sec. vii. for uniformity of service contains the following proviso, "That it shall be lawful for all
" men, as well in Churches, Chapels, Oratories, or
" other places, to use openly any Psalm or Prayer
" taken out of the Bible at any due time, not letting
" or omitting the service or any part thereof men-
" tioned in the said book."—Burn's Eccl. Law, vol. iii. p. 251.

The book of ceremonies, published in 1539, observes—" The sober and discreet devout singing,
" music, and playing with organs, used in the
" Church in the service of God, are ordained to move
" and stir the people to the sweetness of God's word,
" *the which is there sung:* and by that sweet harmony
" both to excite them to prayer and devotion, and
" also to put them in remembrance of the heavenly
" triumphant Church; where is everlasting joy, con-
" tinual laud and praise to God."—page 26.

Queen Elizabeth's Injunctions to the Clergy, 1559, contain the following words—" For the comforting of such as delight in music, it may be permitted, that
" in the beginning or in the end of common prayer,
" either at morning or evening, there may be sung
" an hymn, or such-like song, to the praise of Al-
" mighty God, in the best melody and music that

" may be conveniently devised, having respect that the sentence of the hymn may be understood and perceived."—Sparrow. Collect. Art. Can. 4to. 1684.

The Church of England has abundantly sanctioned the usage of Hymns, by her introduction of the hymn of St. Ambrose, called the Te Deum, the Benedicite, the Gloria in excelsis, and the two metrical versions of the Veni Creator in the Ordination services.

The following selection is partly made from the New Version of the Psalms, in some instances of which a liberty has been taken to alter, to curtail, and to combine, as appeared to the Editor more conducive to edification; some versions are taken from Merrick and other Authors, and the first metres of the first to the fiftieth psalm, are original. To these are annexed the morning and evening Hymns of Bishop Kenn, a version of the *Benedictus*, and *Magnificat*, by Bishop Patrick, the *Benedicite*, abridged from Mr. Merrick, &c.

The second part contains a selection of Psalms and Hymns arranged according to the order of the Book of Common Prayer, for every Sunday in the year, also for the Saint's Days, Holy Communion, and other services.

The *first Psalm* referred to under each Sunday, is the *Psalm* called the *Introit*, as prescribed by the *Rubric* in the reign of King Edw. VI. Some of these Psalms, thus referred to, are not to be found in this Edition; but it is the intention of the Editor, when his time will admit of it, to render the number complete in some future Edition.

The short prefaces to some of the Psalms, viz. the 8th, 15th, 16th, 20th, &c. are abridged from Bishop

Horn's valuable Commentary.—The following observations on the general subject are transcribed from Dr. Tattersall's preface to his Improved Psalmody.—1794.

"Alterations, both partial and general, have already been allowed without ill consequence, and most of the Rulers of the Church have seen and declared the necessity of some further amendment."

Archbishop Secker observes—"It is very true, the verse translation generally used is void of ornament, and hath expressions often low and flat, and sometimes obsolete: I wish a *better* substituted in its place."

Dr. Lowth, late Bishop of London, always honored Mr. Merrick, by corresponding with him on his translation of the Psalms, and furnishing him with his own remarks to forward its success.

Dr. Horne, late Bishop of Norwich, was desirous that the version of Mr. Merrick should be adopted, and introduced several of them into the University Church of St. Mary's, Oxford.

Dr. Wilson, Bishop of Bristol, expressed his earnest wishes to see a good version of the Psalms perfected for the use of a parochial Congregation.

It has been remarked by the Rev. the Dean of Westminster, that in the versification of Sternhold and Hopkins, there are few stanzas which do not give offence. Dr. Brown observes of the New Version of Brady and Tate, that "Though not excellent, it is not intolerable." It has also been remarked, that if Psalmody was once restored to its original rank and estimation, it would become an object of regard to the ruling powers, to have this whole matter re-considered and revised, and that in that case it would not be difficult to form a collection from different

Authors, which would do honor to our own, or any other Church. Such a collection also might be acceptable to the retirement of domestic life, and assist the Master of a family in the high gratification of seeing his children and dependants form a choir to the glory of their Creator and Redeemer.—Dr. Vincent's Considerations on parochial Music, 1787.

The perfection of Church Psalmody consists in the union of the whole Congregation in this important part of worship; and in order thereto, the Psalmody should be plain and simple. The tunes should be harmonious, but not complex; partial repetitions, various notes to express single words, and fugues, are generally unintelligible to the bulk of congregations.

The old Church Melodies supply the finest standard and examples of congregational Music. Such compositions as the 100th Psalm, the 84th and others, are most adapted for public worship. While they exhibit a dignity and melody, which the most eminent Masters of music have acknowledged, they possess also a perspicuity, a simplicity, which renders them attainable by the humble worshipper, and a pathos, solemnity and sublimity, which cannot but interest congregational worship.

Light, airy, theatrical tunes are totally unsuitable to the dignity and simplicity of a Christian Church. Different subjects of Psalmody may require more pathetic, more solemn, or more animated strains of music, but levity is to be avoided. Interchanges of loud and soft music, the *forte* and the *piano*, have a fine effect, relieve the ear and give emphasis to the expression; and it would greatly heighten the effect, if the voices of the men singers, which are so essentially important to swell the chorus, were moderated, or wholly silent in the softer, or *piano* strains, in which the voices of the women and the children should alone be distinctly heard.

Another great injury to Church Psalmody frequently arises from the Charity Children; the evil is almost every where complained of. They are too apt to sing at the utmost height of their voices, the effect of which is general disgust; whereas, if the children were instructed to moderate their voices, their joining in this service would be affecting, delightful and edifying.

Occasional practices of Psalmody in the week-day, or half an hour before the beginning of service, attended by the Minister, or some judicious superintendant, might greatly contribute to the improvement of this important part of worship; and might, by the divine blessing, render it more interesting and edifying to the congregation at large.

It is also submitted to consideration, whether reverence and devotion would not be more strongly marked, if the congregation was instructed to rise and *stand*, when they sung the praises of God. St. Basil, speaking of the Christian Church in his time, says, " The people rising from prayer, *stand up* to sing praise."—Compare also 2 Chron. vii. 6.—Nehemiah ix. 5.—Isaiah vi. 2, 3.—Rev. vii. 9, 10.

The following selection only professes an humble attempt to the improvement of general Church Psalmody, and should it excite any one of more leisure and ability to direct his attention to this important object, the Compiler will be abundantly gratified.

That we may sing with the spirit and with the understanding also, is the humble and fervent prayer of the Editor.   B. W.

See also British Critic, Jan. 1798, page 98.

PSALM.		PSALM.		PSALM.	
1	L. M.	36	L. M.	97	L. M.
2	C. M.	37	S. M.	98	C. M.
3	L. M.	38	L. M.	99	S. M.
4	C. M.	39	C. M.	100	L. M.
5	C. M.	39	2 M. C. M.	100.	2 Metre.
6	C. M.	40	L. M.	103	L. M.
7	L. M.	40	2 M. 7. 7.	103	S. M.
8	L. M,	41	S. M.	104	L. M.
8	2nd part.	41	C. M.	105	C. M.
9	L. M.	42	L. M.	106	L. M,
10	C. M.	42	C. M.	107	L. M.
11	C. M.	43	L. M.	107	C. M.
12	C. M.	44	L. M.	108	C. M.
13	C. M.	45	L. M.	110	C. M.
14	L. M.	46	P. M.	110	2 Metre
15	S. M.	47	C. M.	111	L. M.
16	L. M.	48	L. M.	112	L. M.
16	2nd part.	48	S. M.	113	P. M.
17	L. M.	49	7. 7.	116	C. M.
18	L. M.	50	P. M.	117	D. M.
19	C. M.	51	L. M.	118	C. M.
19	L. M.	57	L. M.	121	C. M.
20	L. M.	63	P. M.	122	P. M.
21	L. M.	63	2 M. L. M.	125	C. M.
22	L. M.	65	L. M.	126	P. M.
23	S. M.	65	2nd part.	130	C. M.
23	2 Metre.	67	S. M.	132	C. M.
23	3 Metre.	68	L. M,	133	P. M.
24	C. M.	71	C. M.	134	C. M.
25	C. M.	71	2 part. C.M.	135	C. M.
25	2nd part.	72	L. M.	136	L. M.
26	C. M.	76	P. M.	138	L. M.
27	L. M.	84	C. M.	139	L, M.
27	2 Metre.	84	2 Metre.	142	S. M.
28	C. M.	86	C. M.	145	C, M.
29	P. M.	89	L. M.	145	2 part. C.M
30	L. M.	90	C. M.	146	C. M.
31	S. M.	91	P. M.	147	L. M.
32	L. M.	92	L. M.	148	C. M.
33	C. M.	93	L. M.	148	P. M.
34	P. M.	95	L. M.	149	old 104th.
34	2 M. C. M.	95	2 Metre.	150	P. M.
35	L. M.				

THE PSALMS OF DAVID.

PSALM I. *(L. M.)*

The blessedness of the righteous.

1 BLEST is the man whose heav'n-taught mind
Disdains the paths which scorners find,
The Law of GOD, his chief delight
He meditates by day and night.

2 Like some fair tree with clust'ring fruit,
Where richest soil supports its root;
No fatal blast its bud attends;
Its fruit in sure perfection ends.

3 Thrice happy man! his branch shall rise,
Stored with rich foliage to the skies;
With streams supplied, from injury free,
'Till glory crown the fruitful tree.

4 The ungodly are to woe consign'd,
Swept like the chaff before the wind;
While saints rejoice to endless days,
GOD hears their prayers, and knows their ways.

PSALM II. (C. M.)

Appointed by the Church for Easter-Day: the opposition of Jew and Gentile against the Messiah—his victory and exaltation. Compare Acts iv. 25.

1 WHY do the nations furious rage?
　　Why vain attempts combine?
　Kings of the earth against the LORD,
　　And His ANOINTED join.

2 He, who in heav'n sits, derides:
　　He bids their wrath be still,
　" MESSIAH, I have made my King
　" On Zion's holy hill."

3 Hear the decree!—Jehovah speaks,
　　" This day, my equal SON,
　" In homage every knee shall bow,
　　" And Thy dominion own."

4 " Ask; and the utmost parts of earth
　　Thine heritage shall be:
　The heathen lands shall own Thee LORD,
　　And be possess'd by Thee."

5 Be wise now therefore, O ye kings,
　　Serve ye the LORD with fear,
　Seek peace with Him, His sceptre own;
　　His pow'r and grace revere.

6 On His great day, His foes shall feel
　　The terror of His word;
　Then, O how blest, thrice blest are they,
　　Who trust in CHRIST the LORD.

PSALM III. *(L. M)*

A Psalm of David, when he fled from Absalom his son, expressing his great confidence and security in God's protection.

1 LORD, how are they increased, who rise
In numbers great, in malice strong!
Bent to destroy, combined, they rage,
With pow'rful hand, with venom'd tongue.

2 But Thou, O LORD, art still my shield,
My buckler, tho' distrest and low;
Do Thou with glory crown my head,
Do thou subdue the cruel foe.

3 Thy mercy doth my soul sustain,
In former straits so oft exprest;
I cried to Thee; nor cried, in vain;
Thou heard'st from heaven; and I was blest.

4 Peaceful to sleep I give my eyes,
In Thee, my FATHER, I confide;
Preserved by Thee, from sleep I rise,
Nor fear ten-thousand foes beside.

5 Rise, Sovereign GOD! salvation shew,
Salvation doth to GOD belong!
Be calm, my soul, surmount thy woe,
And praise JEHOVAH in thy song.

PSALM IV. *(C. M.)*
The same subject continued.

1 O GOD of truth and righteousness,
Attend my cry to Thee!
In former scenes and sad distress
Thou hast delivered me.

PSALM 5.

2 Have mercy, LORD, and hear my prayer;
  My trust is in thy name.
Save me from those, who seek to turn
  My glory into shame.

3 Know that the LORD hath set apart,
  He hears; and he defends,
The godly man, who trusts in Him,
  And on His grace depends.

4 Then stand in awe; sin not; and learn
  To tremble at His word;
Explore thy heart, hope and be still;
  And wait upon the LORD.

5 In vain the sons of men enquire,
  Who, who will shew us good?
Ah! fix on Thee my soul's desire,
  Feed me with heavenly food.

6 With light of thy salvation, LORD,
  O let me thus be blest;
'Tis joy divine, far more than gold,
  Or a whole world possest,

7 Replenish'd, fed, protected, blest;
  What more can I desire?
Thy name, Thy all-sufficient word
  Gladness of heart inspire.

8 Peaceful amidst surrounding foes,
  I'll lay me down to sleep.
Great Guardian, with thy watchful eyes
  My soul in safety keep.

PSALM V.

1 PONDER my words, O LORD, give ear,
  My meditations weigh;

PSALM 5.

O hear my voice, my God, my King,
 To Thee, to Thee, I pray.

2 Before the morning, Thou shalt hear,
 My voice ascending high;
To Thee for refuge I'll look, up;
 My God, hear Thou my cry.

3 O righteous Judge, before Thy throne
 The sinner can not stand;
The workers of iniquity
 Shall tremble at Thy hand

4 No evil, no deceitful men
 Shall ever dwell with Thee;
None without holiness, O Lord,
 Thy face in bliss shall see..

5 But as for me, with holy fear,
 Encouraged by Thy grace,
Thy holy temple I'll approach,
 And bow before Thy face,

6 Lord! lead me in Thy righteousness;
 Guard me from ev'ry snare;
Make plain Thy path before mine eyes;
 Protect me by Thy care.

7 Let all, who trust in God rejoice,
 Secure in His defence;
Let all, who love His name, adore
 His pow'r, His providence.

8 His saints the mighty Lord will save,
 Protected from above,
Bless'd with His favor and te shield
 Of His almighty love.

PSALM 6 & 7.

PSALM VI. (C. M.)

Usually called the first penitential Psalm; it contains confession of sin, application for pardon, and hope of mercy.

1 LORD, in Thy wrath rebuke me not:
   Thine anger, LORD, withdraw!
My soul, oppress'd with sin and grief,
   Adores Thy righteous Law.

2 Tho' by that Law condemn'd, most just
   The sentence, LORD, I own;
Death I deserve; yet grant me life,
   In honor of Thy SON.

3 With self-abhorrence, day and night,
   I grieve, and weep, and pray.
LORD, hear my moan; accept my tears;
   Remove my guilt away.

4 Have mercy, LORD, My SAVIOUR died!
   Mercy's my only plea:
Save me, O LORD, for mercy's sake;
   That mercy shew to me.

5 My soul revives:—My SAVIOUR speaks;
   His pardoning voice I hear!
The LORD hath granted my request,
   The LORD receives my prayer.

6 To Thee, my kind, forgiving GOD
   I'll consecrate my days;
And e'en in death will I proclaim
   The glory of thy grace

PSALM VII (L. M.)

David, persecuted by Cush the Benjamite vindicates his integrity, and refers his cause to his God.

O LORD, my GOD, in Thee I trust;
On Thee alone Thy saints depend.

Psalm 8.

Oppressed by men, unkind, unjust,
  O let Thy pow'r, Thine arm defend.

2 They, who reject Thy righteous Laws,
  Me, for Thy sake, indignant hate;
Combin'd, they seek to crush Thy cause,
  And for the righteous lie in wait.

3 Arise, eternal Lord, arise,
  Defend Thy saints, whom Thou dost love;
Subdue with power Thine enemies
  And let Thy love the weapon prove.

4 Thou most provok'd, yet mighty God,
  Thou strong, yet patient Deity!
Full of forbearance day by day,
  And most long suff'ring, e'en to me!

5 Bless Thou mine enemies; their heart
  Convert by Thine all-powerful word—
Do Thou Thy gracious aid impart,
  Ere yet they fall beneath Thy sword.

6 Thus shall I all Thy gracious ways
  Of justice, mercy, truth proclaim;
And foes with friends in Christ unite,
  And join to praise Thy glorious name.

Psalm VIII. (L. M.)

Appointed by the Church for Ascension Day. It describes the glory of God magnified by his works and by his love to man; and has a spiritual reference to the exaltation of our nature in Messiah, the Second Adam, crowned with glory and honor, and having all things put in subjection under his feet. 1 Cor. xv. 27.—Heb. ii. 5, &c.

1 O LORD, our Lord, how great Thy Name,
  Through earth and heav'ns extensive frame,

Psalm 8.

How dazzling, how divinely great
The glories, which around thee wait.

Praise, endless praise, to Thee belongs,
Ordain'd from babes' and infants' tongues;
Ordain'd Thine honors hence to draw,
And enemies to strike with awe.

When I behold Thy works divine,
When moon and stars around me shine,
LORD what is man! a child of woe,
Yet honor'd and exalted so.

Tenants of earth, and air, and sea,
Own His dominion, and obey.
O LORD, how excellent Thy Name,
Through earth and heav'ns extensive frame!

PART II. (L. M.)

5 LORD, what is man! the pow'r of sin
Left him condemn'd, cast out, unclean,
LORD, what is man! mysterious love
From heav'n stoop'd down to raise above.

6 GOD's everlasting, equal SON,
Both GOD and MAN, in person one,
In human nature was array'd,
And lower than the angels made.

7 Sing of his dying love; and tell,
He rose; he triumph'd, when he fell;

PSALM 9.

As Conq'ror now in bliss enthron'd,
With glory bright, and honor crown'd.

8 Our nature still is his abode;
As man he holds the pow'r of GOD.
All earth and heav'n Him LORD shall own,
The Saviour, GOD, and GOD THE SON.

PSALM IX. (L. M.)

The language of praise, celebrating the victories gained by David; and foretelling the spiritual triumphs of Messiah.

1 WITH my whole heart my GOD I'll praise;
  His marv'llous work my soul proclaim.
His majesty and pow'r I'll sing,
  Exulting in his sacred name.

2 Destruction to its end shall come,
  The humbled foe shall sink to dust
But Thy eternal throne shall last
  For ever glorious, firm and just.

3 Thy mighty power, Thy grace and love,
  To them, who know and trust Thy name,
A refuge, an asylum prove,
  Both now and evermore the same.

4 Sing to the LORD JEHOVAH, sing,
  Who dwells in Zion his abode.
Shew forth his praise throughout her gates;
  The astonish'd world shall own our GOD.

5 Arise, O Lord, convince Thy foes;
  The honor of Thy arm maintain.
No mortal pow'r can Thee oppose,
  And none shall seek Thy face in vain.

PSALM X. (C. M.)

The Church complaining of her enemies, and desponding, prays for protection, and through faith rejoiceth in tribulation

1 WHY standest Thou far off, O Lord?
  Why dost Thou hide Thy face?
My enemies increase, behold
  Thy servant in distress.

2 How awful is the state of men,
  Who dare deride Thy grace!
Thy sacred laws they set at nought,
  And hate Thy holy ways!

3 Arise, O Lord, lift up Thy hand
  From Thy eternal seat;
Command Thine enemies to fall,
  Submissive at Thy feet.

4 Inspire the nations of the world
  With reverence, awe, and fear;
Prepare our hearts to call on Thee,
  And cause Thine ear to hear.

5 Jehovah reigns, for ever reigns!
  The orphan, the oppress'd
Shall learn to trust His sacred name,
  With God's protection bless'd.

PSALM XI. (C. M.)

David, persecuted by Saul, encourages himself in God, his providence and justice.

1 IN Thee, O Lord, I put my trust,
  Why, therefore should I flee?
While hosts of enemies conspire,
  My refuge is in Thee.

PSALM 12.

2 Religion, law, and equity
  They study to erase;
Distress and trial aim to crush
  The basis of my peace.

3 Unto Thy holy temple, LORD,
  Repairs my fearful soul.
Firm as the heav'ns, thy stedfast word
  Can ev'ry heart controul.

4 Trials, commissioned by Thy love,
  Are mercies sent by Thee;
Whilst to the refuge of Thy grace
  Thy saints encouraged flee.

  ehold the wicked; all their ways
  To swift destruction tend;
But GOD, who loveth righteousness,
  The righteous will defend.

PSALM XII. (C. M.)

The Church lamenting the decrease of the righteous, and the increase of sin, is encouraged by the truth and certainty of the promises of God.

1 O LORD, arise and help Thy Church!
    Behold, the godly cease,
  Justice declines; the faithful fail;
    Iniquities increase.

2 Proud in their blasphemies and sins,
    In vanities and lies,
  They dare insult Thy holy word,
    Thy sacred truth despise.

3 But LORD, salvation is with Thee,
    Nor shall Thy foes prevail.
  Thy word of promise stands confess'd,
    Thy Church shall never fail.

PSALM 13.

Pure is Thy word, as silver tried,
  The test hath oft' been made;
Deliv'rance to Thy saints is sure,
  E'en when it seems delay'd.

Thou, LORD, wilt ever keep Thy saints.
  Their cause Thou mak'st Thy own:
The faith, that's built upon Thy word
  Shall ne'er be overthrown

PSALM XIII. (C M.)

A complaint of desertion; a prayer for assistance:—an act of faith and thanksgiving.

HOW long wilt Thou forget me, LORD?
  How long shall I complain?
Cast down, I cry,—Hide not Thy face,
  Nor let me cry in vain.

My fear and sorrows, sins and grief
  Oppress my lab'ring breath;
Consider, LORD; O hear my prayer,
  Lest I should sleep in death.

Let not my enemies rejoice,
  Or triumph in my fall,
Lest they reproach Thy holy ways,
  And say, in vain I call.

In Thy salvation, LORD, I'll hope,
  So oft I've proved thy pow'r;
Thy grace I'll sing, Thy goodness tell,
  In this distressing hour.

To Thee, my SAVIOUR, bounteous GOD
  My grateful song I'll raise,
And trust Thy mighty pow'r to save,
  Till prayer's absorb'd in praise.

PSALM XIV. *(L. M.)*

The Church lamenting the depravity of man, longeth for the Redemption of Christ.

THERE is a God all nature cries;
  None but the fool the truth denies.
On all God's works it stands exprest,
By vivid arguments confest.

From heav'n the Mighty Lord look'd down,
From heav'n, his high exalted throne,
Enquiring on this world's abode,
Who understands and seeks their God?

From His appointed righteous way,
Alas! they all are gone astray,
The ways of peace they have not known;
And none is righteous; no, not one.

Guilty, condemn'd, deprav'd and lost,
Who before God hath ought to boast?
Arise, O King of Sion, rise,
And bring salvation from the skies.

Then shall Thy saints rejoice and sing,
And each glad heart its tribute bring.
Pardon and peace shall then be given;
And thousands soar from earth to heav'n.

PSALM XV. *(S M)*

Appointed by the Church for Ascension Day— as exhibiting the character of the Prince and Citizens of Zion.

WHO shall ascend and dwell
  With Thee, Almighty God?
Who shall in Zion's holy hill
  Inhabit Thine abode?

PSALM 16.

2. He, who is pure in heart,
    Whose words and thoughts are one
  Whose will is to God's will conform'd,
    Whose feet obedient run.

3 Who never with design
    Would hurt another's fame;
  But to promote his happiness,
    His universal aim.

4 Who sin in every form,
    In every rank reproves;
  But them, who serve and fear the Lord,
    Honors, esteems, and loves.

5 Who, faithful to his word,
    His lips with truth adorns;
  Who pleads the cause of innocence,
    And mean advantage scorns.

6 These works, effects of faith,
    Labors of active love,
  Here glorify God's Name and meet
    Rewards of grace above.

6 Such was the Son of God,
    Mirror of truth and grace!
  Seek to do good like him on earth,
    In heav'n behold his face.

PSALM XVI. (L. M.)

David describing his own distress and hope of eternal life, prophecies of the death, resurrection and glory of Messiah.—Compare Acts ii 25. & xiii. 35

1 PRESERVE me, Lord, in Thee I trust,
    To Thine almighty arm I flee.

PSALM 16.

My goodness no returns can make,
   Nor can extend, my God, to Thee.

O condescension great, which deigns
   Our humble services to own,
And acts of kindness shewn Thy saints,
   Acknowledges before Thy throne.

Tho' oft by sinful man despis'd,
   Esteem'd, and valued in Thy sight,
In them Thine image, Lord, I see;
   In them as excellent delight.

Be Thou the portion of my cup;
   My God, my heritage, my all,
O fix my stedfast eyes on Thee;
   Protect and guard me, lest I fall.

Lord, when in dust I lay my head,
   My fading flesh in hope shall rest,
By pow'r divine, ere long, reviv'd,
   Shall rise triumphant, pure and blest.

The path of life my eyes shall see,
   In Thy blest presence Thee adore.
Fulness of joy's at Thy right hand,
   Glory and pleasures evermore.

PART II. *(L. M.)*

PRESERVE me, Lord, the Saviour cried.
   My soul, remark his dying groan!
Upon the cross, He bleeds, He dies
   Dies for transgressions not his own.

His pure obedience unto death
   Extended not Himself to bless.
A mantle to his saints it proved,
   A robe of spotless righteousness.

3 Glory to Thee, O LAMB of GOD!
   Thy sacred blood atonement made,
Be Thou my portion, Thou my hope,
   By Thee the debt of sin was paid.

4 At Thy right hand JEHOVAH stood.
   Thy pow'r atchiev'd the arduous plan.
In the dark grave GOD's HOLY ONE
   Repos'd, and rescued fallen man.

5 The path of life, before untried,
   To Thee was shewn, by Thee explor'd.
O mystery great! man thus enjoys
   Pleasures for ever with his LORD.

PSALM XVII.   (L. M.)

A prayer for divine protection and guidance, in the confidence of hope.

1 HEAR Thou my right, O LORD, attend,
   FATHER of all, my soul defend.
While enemies around me tread,
Deign Thou my humble cause to plead.

2 O Thou, my GOD, my guard, my guide,
Leave not my erring feet to slide.
Hold Thou my footsteps in Thy way,
Prove Thou my heart, nor let me stray.

3 Thy marv'lous loving-kindness shew;
Let Thy right hand disarm the foe;
Protect and keep me, King of kings,
Under the shadow of Thy wings.

4 On Thee I call, O LORD, arise;
Oft Thou, my GOD, hast heard my cries;
Thy mighty arm the foe can quell,
And their united pow'rs repel.

PSALM 18.

5 As Lions, greedy of their prey,—
Bent to destroy, they watch my way;
Invidious, circling me around,
My steps they mark, my paths surround.

6 Arise, O Lord, perform Thy word,
The wrath of man is but Thy sword!
Far other joys my eyes behold
Than this life's bliss, or sordid gold.

7 O grant me to behold Thy face,
In realms of righteousness and peace;
Thy image there shall I partake,
And fully satisfied awake.

PSALM XVIII. *(L M.)*

A song of victory, in the day that the Lord had delivered David out of the hand of all his enemies, and out of the hand of Saul—2 Sam. xxii. 1, &c. It contains a magnificent description of divine interposition, deliverance and victory. The 49th verse is applied by St. Paul to the conversion of the Gentiles.—Rom. xv. 9.

1 THEE will I love, O Lord, my strength,
   My rock, protector, and my God;
My buckler, my salvation Thou,
   My fortress, my secure abode.

2 To Thee, oppress'd, I made my prayer;
   All might, all praise to Thee belongs.
The vanquish'd enemy retreats—
   And vict'ry swells our grateful songs.

3 In our distress on God we call'd;
   The enemy beheld and fear'd.

PSALM 19.

Gigantic in his circuit seen,
  Rejoicing in his might.

The gladden'd world with joy beholds,
  The splendor of its rise;
Emblem of God, of grace and truth,
  The glory of the skies.

The Law of God converts the soul,
  Diffusing nobler light;
Its influence makes the simple wise,
  The blind restores to sight.

How perfect is thy Law, O God,
  How pure the sacred word;
How holy, righteous, just and good,
  The judgements of the Lord!

O precious more than finest gold,
  The knowledge of the Lord!
O sweeter far than honey comb,
  The sweetness of thy word!

By this Thy servant, timely warn'd,
  Escapes the snares of sin.
By these instructions daily taught,
  Preserves his conscience clean.

O who can count his num'rous faults?
  Who can his heart explore?
Lord, keep me from presumptuous sin,
  Lest I offend Thee more.

O may the musing of my heart,
  My ev'ry thought and word,
Accepted alway be by Thee,
  My strength, Redeemer, Lord.

PSALM XIX. II. METRE.

1 THE spacious firmament on high,
With all the blue etherial sky,
And spangled heav'ns, a shining frame,
Their great original proclaim.
Th' unwearied sun, from day to day,
Does his Creator's pow'r display,
And publishes to ev'ry land
The work of an almighty hand.

2 Soon as the ev'ning shades prevail,
The moon takes up the wondrous tale,
And nightly to the list'ning earth
Repeats the story of her birth,
Whilst all the stars that round her burn,
And all the planets in their turn,
Confirm the tidings as they roll,
And spread the truth from pole to pole.

3 What though in solemn silence all
Move round the dark terrestrial ball?
What though nor real voice nor sound
Amid the radiant orbs be found?
In reason's ear they all rejoice,
And utter forth a glorious voice,
For ever singing as they shine,
'The hand that made us is divine.'

PSALM XX. (L. M.)

The Church prayeth for the prosperity of King Messiah, going forth to the battle as her Champion, Deliverer and High Priest; blesseth the King in his exploits, and expresses confidence in his Salvation.

1 IN Thy distress the LORD attend,
The name of Jacob's GOD defend;

Sustain thee in thy trying hour,
And succour with almighty pow'r.

Go, Captain of Salvation,! go,
Perfect thro' suff'ring made below;
Thy God thy agonies relieve,
And Thy grand sacrifice receive.

God shall supply thy every want,
Thine hearts desire fulfil, and grant;
By Thee to bliss shall millions rise,
Lo! countless trophies grace the skies.

Messiah's heard; the work is done;
The great Salvation's all Thy own!
Our banners we exulting raise;
Thine all the glory! Thine the praise!

Triumphant in Thy sacred name,
All other refuge we disclaim;
By Thee upheld; by Thee we rise;
Thy name our passport to the skies.

They, who thy grace refuse, shall fall,
Lord save us, hear us, when we call.
Let saints in earth, and heav'n proclaim
Endless Hosannas to Thy name.

PSALM XXI.

Appointed by the Church for Ascension Day, celebrating the victory and glory of the Redeemer, his kingdom and final triumph.

THE king shall in Thy strength rejoice,
O Lord of Hosts, with grateful voice;
Salvation's glorious work is done;
Let heav'n and earth the triumph own.

PSALM 21.

2 His heart's desire, divine request!
Man to redeem, condemn'd, opprest;
Blessings of goodness hence are spread,
And purest gold adorns his head.

3 He asked life: and life was giv'n,
Eternal, as the days of heav'n,
His glories in Salvation shine,
Honor and majesty divine.

4 Ye saints, ye angels hov'ring round,
Behold the great Messiah, crown'd;
Enter'd within the promis'd rest,
For ever, and for ever, blest.—

5 O life divine! inspiring word!
As man He trusted in the Lord;
He died; He rose; He left the grave,
Glorious in pow'r, and strong to save.

6 Thine enemies shall feel thy hand;
Destruction waits thy dread command;
Beneath Thy wrath Thy foes consume,
And own the justice of their doom.

6 Exalted high, rise, mighty Lord,
Thy strength display; unsheath thy sword,
Live, live, and reign to endless days,
Thy greatness, and thy pow'r we praise.

N. B. This Psalm may be sung to the tune of the 23rd Psalm, 3rd metre; by adding these two lines to every stanza,—

Glory to God, Messiah reigns;
O praise Him, praise in endless strains!

PSALM XXII. (L. M.)

Appointed by the Church for Good Friday. The first verse was uttered by our Lord, when hanging on the Cross. It describes his sufferings, humiliation and glory; and prophecieth the conversion of the Gentiles to the faith and worship of the true God.

MY God, my God, Messiah cried,
When on the cross He bled and died,
Ah! why exil'd my God from Thee?
Ah! why hast Thou forsaken me!

With agony oppress'd I faint;
By day, by night incessant pant,
O'erwhelm'd with anguish, pain and grief,
O why so far from my relief?

Yet just and good Thy ways I own,
Thou perfect, righteous, holy One.
Thy glory from this cross shall shine,
And praise, eternal praise, be Thine.

Our fathers trusted in thy word,
When, when were they forsaken Lord?
O pity, hear thy servant then,
Rejected, and despised of men.

Ye that pass by, the scene behold,
Contemplate grief and love untold;
The Son of God on Calv'ry's tree,
Forsaken, bleeding, dying see.

For man a crown of thorns He wears,
The nail, the spear His body tears,
See streaming blood His form disguise,
Hark! His last words,—He groans, He dies.

7 See inward terrors melt His heart!
See ruffian hands His garments part!
O Lord of strength, Thy suff'rer own,
Immanuel, Thy united one.*

8 O mystery great of love divine!
Justice and grace emblazon'd shine.
Glory to God from hence shall spring,
And heav'n with Hallelujahs ring.

9 The Saviour lives; — lives to proclaim,
Jehovah's glorious awful name
Let the great congregation raise,
His grace and truth above all praise.

10 Ye seed of Jacob's honor'd race,
Your anthems bring, the triumph grace;
Ye seed of Israel, join your songs;
Praise Him, to whom all praise belongs.

11 O glorify and fear the Lord,
Who in distress confirms His word;
Nor hides His face; nor turns His eye;
From deep affliction's plaintive cry.

12 Trust Him ye meek, partake His feast
Provided by your great High Priest,
Who seek the Lord, with Him shall rise,
And live for ever in the skies.

13 The heathen lands shall own their God,
Repent and turn to His abode,
Receive His soul-reviving words,
The King of kings, the Lord of lords

14 The rich, the great ones of the earth,
No more shall boast their wealth or birth,

PSALM 23.

But crowding round His festive board,
Prostrate adore their sov'reign LORD.

15 The dead shall rise, and bow the knee;
Yea; ev'ry eye the Judge shall see;
Millions of people yet unborn,
Shall rise His triumphs to adorn.

16 A seed shall come, and learn thy word,
A generation to the LORD,
The Gentiles, yet far off, shall raise,
Anthems of glory to thy praise.

17 The heathen lands shall bless Thy name,
Thy truth, Thy righteousness proclaim,
Yea; all shall come, adore and own,
This mightiest work the LORD hath done.

PSALM XXIII. (S. M.)

The guardian care of the Good Shepherd in feeding, restoring, conducting, defending, and replenishing the sheep of his pasture, through time to the blissful glories of eternity.

1 MY Shepherd is the LORD,
   I never more shall want;
All I require my gracious GOD,
   Will mercifully grant.

2 In meadows fair and green,
   With purest pasture blest;
Where the still waters gently flow,
   He leadeth me to rest.

3 When from Thy paths I err,
   My GOD, my soul restore,
Lead me in paths of righteousness,
   That I may stray no more.

PSALM 23.

4 In gloomy shades of death,
   Then shall I fear no ill;
Thy staff and sceptre comfort me,
   And Thou art with me still.

5 In presence of my foes,
   My table Thou dost spread;
My cup with mercy overflows;
   Thine oil anoints my head.

Thy goodness, mercy, peace,
   Shall follow all my days;
And in thy house I'll ever dwell,
   And sing Thy ceaseless praise.

PSALM XXIII. II. Metre. *Old Version. (C.M.)*

1 MY Shepherd is the living LORD.
   Nothing therefore I need;
In pastures fair, near pleasant streams,
   He setteth me to feed.

2 He shall convert and glad my soul,
   And bring my mind in frame,
To walk in paths of righteousness,
   For His most holy name.

3 Yea, tho' I walk in vale of death
   Yet I will fear no ill;
Thy rod and staff do comfort me,
   And Thou art with me still.

4 And in the presence of my foes
   My table Thou shalt spread;
Thou wilt fill full my cup, and Thou
   Anointed hast my head.

PSALM 23.

5 Though all my life, Thy favour is
   So frankly shewn to me,
That in Thy house for evermore
   My dwelling-place shall be.

PSALM XXIII. III. METRE. *(L M)*

1 THE LORD my pasture shall prepare,
   And feed me with a shepherd's care:
His presence shall my wants supply,
And guard me with a watchful eye;
My noon-day walks he shall attend,
And all my midnight hours defend.

2 When in the sultry glebe I faint,
Or on the thirsty mountain pant,
To fertile vales and dewy meads
My weary wand'ring steps he leads,
Where peaceful rivers, soft and slow,
Amid the verdant landscape flow.

3 Though in the paths of death I tread,
With gloomy horrors overspread,
My stedfast heart shall fear no ill;
For Thou, O LORD, art with me still:
Thy friendly crook shall give me aid,
And guide me thro' the dreadful shade.

4 Though in a bare and rugged way,
Thro' devious lonely wilds I stray,
Thy bounty shall my pains beguile;
The barren wilderness shall smile,
With sudden greens and herbage crown'd,
And streams shall murmur all around

PSALM XXIV. (C. M.)

The Ark of God moving in a grand solemn procession to Mount Sion 1 Chron. xv. an emblem of the Christian Church and the glorious Ascension of the Messiah; as such appointed by the Church for Ascension-day.

1 THE earth, and all that dwell therein,
    JEHOVAH owns its LORD,
Form'd on the seas and swelling floods,
    Created by His word.

2 Who shall on high ascend and dwell,
    The holy place of GOD?
The man, whose heart, whose hands are clean
    And meet for Thine abode.

3 The man, who vanity abhors;
    Whose life from guilt is free;
Who scorns deceit, maintains the truth,
    Whose heart is right with Thee.

4 This is the generation, LORD,
    Of such as seek Thy face;
Blessings divine shall they receive,
    Glory and righteousness.

5 Lift up your heads, eternal gates,
    Ye realms of light make room;
Ye everlasting doors, behold
    The King of glory come!

6 Who is the King of glory, who?
    The mighty Chief renown'd;
Mighty in battle, glorious LORD,
    He comes with triumph crown'd.

7 Lift up your heads, eternal gates,
   Unfold the heav'nly scene;
 The King of glory comes;—receive
   The King of glory in.

8 Who is this King of glory who?
   The Lord of Hosts, renown'd,
 All hail!—Messiah is His name,
   The King of glory crown'd.

9 (The Saviour thus was once receiv'd
   By Heav'n's angelic train,
 And thus His faithful saints shall rise,
   And heirs of glory reign.)

PSALM XXV. (C. M.)

A Prayer for pardon, help and protection; and describing the blessedness of the man, who feareth the Lord.

1 TO Thee, O Lord, I lift my soul,
   My God, I trust in Thee;
 Let not mine enemies rejoice,
   Or triumph over me.

2 Shew me Thy paths, teach me Thy truth,
   Direct me in Thy way;
 Thou God of my salvation, hear
   On Thee I wait all day.

3 Call to remembrance, O my God,
   Thy loving kindness past;
 Thy tender mercies, oft of old,
   My anxious fears surpast.

4 Remember not my youthful sins,
   When I transgress'd Thy word;

PSALM 25.

In mercy, for Thy goodness sake,
  Remember me, O Lord.

5 Thou good, and righteous, holy One,
  Thy grace and pardon give.
Teach me to find Thy way, that I
  May to Thy glory live.

6 Divine simplicity of soul,
  Meekness and peace impart,
Instruct my soul; in judgment guide,
  And fix my wav'ring heart.

7 Thy paths of mercy, grace, and truth,
  Sweet peace and joy instil,
To such as do Thy covenant keep,
  Obedient to Thy will.

8 My sin is great; my sin forgive,
  My nature cleanse within;
Thus glorify Thy name, O Lord,
  And pardon all my sin.

PSALM XXV. PART II.

9 O Highly favor'd, happy man,
  The man, who fears the Lord!
Unerring truth shall guide his steps,
  God's providence and word.

10 The blessing of the Lord shall rest
  On him and on his seed,
While sov'reign goodness, love and pow'r,
  Their steps to glory lead.

11 Calmness of mind, and holy fear
  His peace and hope improve;

PSALM 26.

His covenant God to him will shew,
  The counsels of His love.

2 Mine eyes are ever fix'd on Thee;
  O Lord, preserve my feet,
Turn Thou to me, O hear my prayer,
  From heav'n, Thy mercy-seat.

3 The sorrows of my heart enlarge,
  My num'rous foes increase;
O look on my adversity,
  And bid my sorrows cease.

4 Succour and keep my soul, O God,
  In the afflictive hour;
Thou art my hope; Thine Israel guard,
  With Thine almighty pow'r.

PSALM XXVI.   (C M.)

An appeal to God & delight in divine ordinances.

1 JUDGE me, O Lord, my trust art Thou
    Examine, prove my heart,
  Try Thou my reins, that I from Thee
    May never more depart.

2 Thy loving kindness, and Thy truth,
    I set before mine eyes;
  Hence, ye deceitful, who delight
    In vanity and lies.

3 Thine altar, Lord, will I frequent,
    Where all Thy saints repair;
  My soul exults with songs of praise,
    To tell Thy wonders there,

4 My hands I'll wash in innocence,
    By Thine almighty grace,

PSALM 27.

   And hail with gratitude and joy,
     The glories of the place.

5 O how I love Thy sacred courts,
    Where prayer and praise arise!
  There, where Thy honor dwells, I find
    My foretaste of the skies.

6 Lord, with the just appoint my lot,
    To walk Thy holy ways;
  Till, with Thy saints enthron'd on high
    I chaunt eternal praise.

PSALM XXVII.   (L. M.)

Confidence in God in the midst of danger, and triumphant assurance of final Victory.

1 THOU my Salvation art, O Lord,
   My light of truth Thy sacred word;
  Strength of my life, whom shall I fear,
  While Thine almighty arm is near?

2 Tho' hosts of men their weapons wield,
  My heart to terror ne'er shall yield;
  My soul may all their threats despise,
  Guarded by Thee, should wars arise.

3 One grand pursuit my heart inspires,
  Long as I live, my soul desires
  To dwell in Thy belov'd abode,
  To view Thy beauty, O my God.

4 O blest pavilion, where Thy saints
  Relief obtain in all complaints:
  Fix'd on a rock, Thy pow'r they know,
  And rise triumphant o'er the foe.

PSALM 27.

5 Thy praise shall hence my pow'rs employ,
The grateful sacrifice of joy;
Awake my soul, awake my tongue,
Let Hallelujahs swell the song.

6 To Thee I cry: LORD, hear my voice;
Thy answer makes my heart rejoice;
"Seek ye my face." O sacred word!
Thy face I'll seek, most gracious LORD.

7 Ah! hide not Thou Thy face from me,
Till I in bliss Thy glories see;
Be still my succour, still my friend,
GOD of Salvation, to the end.

8 Should friends on earth deceitful prove;
Should parents lose a parent's love.
The parent and the friend I see
More than supplied, my GOD, in Thee.

9 Oft had I fainted, but Thy name,
Faithful, unchangeable, the same,
Taught me to look beyond the grave,
And trust Thy sov'reign pow'r to save.

10 Wait on the LORD in ev'ry strait;
Be strong in faith; in patience wait;
Thine heart He strengthens; trust His word;
O wait for ever on the LORD

PSALM XXVII. II. METRE. *(L, M.)*

1 THOU, LORD, my safety, Thou my light.
What danger shall my soul affright?
Strength of my life! what arm shall dare
To hurt whom Thou hast own'd Thy care?

PSALM 28.

2 One wish, with holy transport warm,
My heart has form'd, and yet shall form;
One gift I ask; that to my end
Thy sacred courts I may attend.

3 There may I find a sure abode,
And view the beauty of my GOD;
For He within His hallow'd shrine
My secret refuge shall assign.

4 When Thou, with condescending grace,
Hast bid me seek Thy shining face,
My heart replied to Thy kind word,
Thee will I seek, all gracious Lord.

5 Should ev'ry earthly friend depart,
And nature leave a parent's heart;
My GOD, on whom my hopes depend,
Will be my Father and my Friend.

6 Ye humble souls, in ev'ry strait,
On GOD with sacred courage wait;
His hand shall life and strength afford,
O ever wait upon the LORD.

PSALM XXVIII. *(C. M.)*

The language of humiliation, intercession & triumph.

1 TO Thee I cry, O LORD, my rock,
Thine arm alone can save.
Ah! be not silent, lest I sink
Forgotten in the grave.

2 The voice of supplication, LORD,
My anxious fears repeat;

PSALM 28.

With ceaseless cries, I lift my hands
  Tow'rds Heav'n, Thy mercy-seat.

3 Ungodly men care not for Thee,
  They from Thy ways depart;
Peace to their neighbour speak their lips,
  With mischief in their heart.

4 Thy works, the glory of Thy hands
  Thy pow'r and skill declare;
Yet sinners' hearts they ne'er attract,
  Nor make impression there.

5 Who serve not God, while here on earth,
  Who care not, Lord, for Thee,
According to their just desert,
  Thy face shall never see.

6 Almighty God, enthron'd on high,
  Thy name be ever blest—
My supplications Thou hast heard,
  And granted my request.

7 O Thou, my confidence, my strength,
  My shield in all distress,
How greatly doth my heart rejoice,
  And Thy salvation bless.

8 Jehovah is our sure defence.
  His pow'r, and grace our theme;
Strength of Messiah, and His Church,
  Of all, who trust in Him.

9 Lord, save Thy people, bless Thy saints;
  Till ev'ry danger's o'er;
With heav'nly manna feed their souls,
  Exalt them evermore.

PSALM XXIX.

The Prophet calleth the Kings of the earth to give glory to Jehovah, and to admire the magnificent effects of his power.

1 BRING to the LORD, the mighty King,
   Your grateful off'rings hither bring,
     Your sacrifice prepare.
Ye kings and rulers of the earth,
Praise Him, to whom you owe your birth,
     His sacred pow'r declare.

2 With holy worship sound His praise;
   To highest heav'ns His honors raise;
     Give glory to His name.
The beauty of His holiness,
In all your themes of praise express,
     And spread abroad His fame.

3 GOD speaks;—the GOD of glory speaks;
   Forth from the skies the lightning breaks;
     The thunder's awful noise.
Earth stands astonish'd at the sound,
The whirlwinds shake, and rend the ground;
     Man trembles at His voice.

4 See! Lebanon's wide desarts shake;
   Behold! the oaks of Kadesh break;
     The crashing cedars rend!
Praise His magnificence of pow'r;
His glory speak; His name adore,
     And in His temple bend.

5 Let oceans wide His wonders tell;
   At GOD's command, the billows swell,
     At GOD's command subside.

PSALM 30.

Combine, ye seas, His name to bless,
Ye raging waves, the God confess;
   Who rules th' impetuous tide

6 God sitteth on the water-flood;
His throne from age to age hath stood;
   His kingdom ne'er shall cease.
Strength to His people God will give;
Their souls will bless; their wants relieve,
   And grant eternal peace.

PSALM XXX. (L. M.)

A Psalm of praise at the dedication of the house of David, celebrating deliverance from sickness and danger, and glorifying God.

THEE will I magnify, O Lord,
   Thy sacred truth, Thy faithful word,
Thy pow'r my enemies supprest,
Pleaded my cause, and gave me rest

O Lord, my God, I cried to Thee;
In mercy Thou hast healed me.
From terror, darkness, and the grave,
Thy mighty arm ordain'd to save.

Give praise, ye saints, with me confess
The mem'ry of His holiness;
His love returns; His anger's past;
His wrath doth but a moment last.

Though grief the night oppress with tears,
The morning dawns, and joy appears;
In His good pleasure life resides,
And bliss eternally abides.

Elated with prosperity,
Removed, we think, we ne'er can be;

PSALM 31.

God turns His face; instant appear
Darkness, and clouds, and sad despair,

6 Taught by distress, to God we flee,
Our refuge in adversity,
And at His feet submissive bow;
By suff'ring taught our God to know.

7 Lord, hear my plea, prolong my days,
And may each day proclaim Thy praise;
Spare me, my God, in mercy spare,
Thy truth, Thy mercy to declare.

8 In great compassion hear my cry,
My helper, God, in trouble nigh;
Swift to my succour mercy flies,
And hope revives, and terror dies.

9 Ye saints, with praise your songs employ,
See heaviness exchang'd for joy;
Mourning put off, with gladness crown'd,
See mercy beaming all around.

10 My tongue, the glory of my frame,
Shall sound aloud Jehovah's name;
Perpetual mercy God displays:
Perpetual themes shall chaunt His praise.

PSALM XXXI. *(S. M.)*

Supplication for deliverance, and gratitude for mercies; the 5th verse was pronounced by our Lord, when expiring on the cross.

1 IN Thee, O Lord, I trust,
 My hope is in Thy name.
In righteousness deliver me,
 Nor put my soul to shame.

PSALM 31.

2 From heav'n bow down thine ear,
 My cause in mercy plead;
My rock, my fortress, my defence,
 My soul vouchsafe to lead.

3 From ev'ry snare preserve;
 From ev'ry foe defend;
For Thy name's sake O God, my strength,
 Divine protection send.

4 Into Thy hands O Lord,
 My spirit I commend;
Thou hast redeem'd me, God of truth;
 In death be Thou my friend.

5 I will be glad and praise;
 And in Thy name rejoice;
In sorrow Thou hast known my soul,
 And heard my plaintive voice.

6 My trouble still regard;
 My God my fears controul,
My eye consumes, my spirit faints,
 My body and my soul.

7 My life is spent with grief,
 In sighing pass my years;
My strength consumes because of sin,
 In grief, distress, and tears.

8 Reproach'd, cast out, despis'd,
 By friends, by foes oppress'd;
Harrass'd with fears, on ev'ry side,
 Forsaken, and distress'd.

9 But still Thou art my God,
 Although by man abhor'd,
Thou the asylum of my soul,
 My trust is in Thy word.

PSALM 31.

10 My times are in Thy hand,
   My great almighty friend.
 When persecuting foes combine,
   Do Thou my soul defend.

11 O grant me to behold,
   Thy power, Thy truth, Thy grace;
 Lord, for Thy mercy's sake display
   The brightness of Thy face.

12 Thy goodness, O how great,
   Eternally the same!
 Before the sons of men laid up,
   For those who fear thy name.

13 Thy presence shall protect,
   Thy watchful care shall hide;
 In the pavilion of Thy love
   Secure Thy saints abide.

14 For ever bless the Lord,
   His great Salvation tell.
 His marv'lous loving kindness keeps
   The city, where we dwell.

15 Despond not of His truth,
   Nor yield to anxious grief;
 God heard my voice, when in distress
   I sought and found relief.

16 O love the Lord, ye saints,
   The faithful God will guard;
 Sin He will punish; but the just
   In mercy will reward.

17 Be of good courage then,
   Establish'd on His word;

Your heart he strengthens; trust His name,
And triumph in the LORD.

PSALM XXXII. (L. M.)

The second penitential Psalm; true blessedness consisteth in remission of sins, the character and encouragement of true repentance. St. Paul applies it to illustrate our justification, Rom. iv. 6. 7. 8.

1 BLEST is the man, O, blest of heav'n,
  Whose sins are pardon'd by his GOD;
All whose transgressions are forgiv'n
  And cover'd with atoning blood.

2 To him the LORD no sin imputes;
  His heart is free from guile within,
His works attest his faith sincere;
  True evidence of pardon'd sin.

3 By day and night, with guilt cast down,
  In deep despondency opprest,
Silent I mourn'd my absent GOD,
  And seem'd in vain to seek for rest.

4 I said, I will confess my sin;
  Thou LORD almighty art to save;
My sin confest;—my gracious Lord
  All my iniquities forgave.

5 This act of mercy, Godlike grace,
  Memorial of Thy pard'ning pow'r,
Shall teach Thy saints to Thee to pray,
  Thou refuge in affliction's hour.

6 When billows swell, when tempests rage;
  When the great water-floods prevail,

PSALM 38.

Thy saints upborn, preserv'd by Thee,
   Shall never find Thy mercy fail.

7 My hiding place, secure in Thee,
   No terrors shall my soul annoy;
Songs of deliv'rance Thou shalt raise,
   Encompassing my soul with joy.

8 Guide me with Thine unerring eye,
   Instruct and teach me in Thy way;
Point out the path; direct my soul
   To realms of everlasting day.

9 GOD's service perfect freedom is;
   Be ye not like the horse or mule;
Let gentler means obedience teach,
   And let His Law thy spirit rule.

10 Be glad ye righteous, and rejoice,
   Ye upright souls make GOD your trust,
Great plagues for sinners shall remain;
   Encircling mercy guards the just.

PSALM XXXIII. (C M.)

An exhortation to praise God for His truth, righteousness, mercy and power.

1 REJOICE ye righteous, in the LORD,
   Your songs triumphant raise;
For well the upright it becomes
   To celebrate His praise.

2 With sweetest melody of song,
   JEHOVAH's praise proclaim;
Let music all her pow'rs combine,
   JEHOVAH's praise the theme,

3 His sacred words most just and true
   Life, peace and joy afford;
 Through the wide world His works proclaim,
   The goodness of the Lord.

4 O praise our God, th'eternal Word,
   By whom the heav'ns were made;
 All their grand host his breath ordain'd,
   And earths foundation laid.

5 Wide oceans rise at his command,
   At his command subside;
 In the great deep their bounds he lays,
   And curbs their swelling tide.

6 O fear the Lord, O stand in awe,
   Praise Him while ages last.
 God spake;—the globe in order rose.
   God spake;—and it stood fast.

7 God brings to nought the plans of men,
   Their projects turns to shame;
 But Thy decrees, O Lord, shall stand
   Eternally the same.

3 Bless'd is the nation where the Lord
   Jehovah is their God:
 O happy people, favor'd land,
   Chosen for His abode.

9 From heav'n the mighty God surveys
   The counsels men combine;
 Detects their thoughts, observes their works,
   And governs the design.

10 Without the Lord, the valiant hosts,
    The sword, the shield are vain,
  The horse, the rider, all the strength,
    Of wars terrific train.

PSALM 34.

11 On those, who fear, and trust His pow'r,
   God looks, and, from the skies,
Guards them from death, preserves alive,
   And all their wants supplies.

12 On God, our shield, our souls shall wait;
   His help inspires our voice;
His holy name's our only hope,
   Then let our hearts rejoice.

13 Lord, let Thy mercy on us rest
   Our strength on Thee depends;
Be Thou the anchor of our souls,
   Whose mercy never ends.

PSALM XXXIV.

A song of praise, celebrating great deliverance, exhorting to fear, trust and experience the goodness of Jehovah; composed by David on his escape from Ahimelech.

WITH ceaseless praise I'll bless the Lord,
   His providence and grace record,
     And spread abroad His fame.
In Him my soul shall make her boast,
The humble man shall hear and trust,
     And join the grateful theme.

2 O magnify the Lord with me;
Proclaim His rich benignity,
     Give glory to His name.
I sought the Lord; He heard my cry;
Mercy descended from on high,
     And all my fears o'ercame.

PSALM 34.

3 The saints of God beheld and learn'd,
 The myst'ry of His ways discern'd,
  His dispensations bless'd.
 The poor man cried; God heard his prayer,
 Reliev'd his sorrow, sooth'd his care,
  And rescued, when distress'd.

4 Behold! commissioned from on high,
 The guardian armies of the sky,
  The Angel of the Lord;
 O taste and see, that God is love,
 What bliss the happy man doth prove,
  Who fears and trusts His word.

5 The lions roar and suffer want;
 But the great God all good will grant,
  His saints shall be supplied.
 O fear the Lord, fear Him ye saints,
 Pour forth to Him your sad complaints,
  Jehovah will provide.

PART II.

6 O come ye children, come and learn,
 Paths of true happiness discern,
  These sacred precepts hear.
 See glory crown extended days,
 See peace and goodness mark the ways
  Of God's most holy fear!

7 Thy tongue from guile and evil guard;
 Speak the plain truth; all sin discard;
  And to the end endure;
 Depart from evil, and do good;
 For peace, with God and man pursued,
  Will happiness ensure.

PSALM 34. (II. Metre)

8 God hears the righteous when they cry;
  His faithful, His omniscient eye
    Awakes to guard the just.
In God the wicked find no friend,
Their steps to sure destruction tend,
    Their mem'ry sinks in dust.

9 God deigns to hear the humble sigh,
  To such the Lord of hosts is nigh,
    Their tears His pity move;
Tho' many their afflictions be,
E'er long, deliv'rance they shall see,
    And rest eternal prove,

10 His watchful care His saints observes,
  Their body and their soul preserves,
    Their ev'ry want supplies.
Evil the wicked man o'ertakes,
But God His servants ne'er forsakes.
    'Till perfect in the skies.

PSALM XXXIV. II. METRE. New Ver. (C.M.)

1 THRO' all the changing scenes of life,
  In trouble and in joy,
Thy praises, O my God, shall still
  My heart and tongue employ.

2 Of Thy deliv'rance I will boast,
  Till all, who are distrest,
From my example comfort take,
  And charm their griefs to rest.

3 O magnify the Lord with me,
  With me exalt His name;
When in distress to Him I call'd,
  He to my rescue came.

PSALM 35.

4 The hosts of God encamp around
 The dwellings of the just;
Deliv'rance He affords to all,
 Who on His succour trust.

5 O make but trial of His love,
 Experience will decide
How bless'd they are, and only they,
 Who on His truth confide.

6 Fear Him, ye saints, and you will then
 Have nothing else to fear;
Make you His service your delight,
 He'll make your wants His care

PSALM XXXV. *(L. M.)*

This Psalm, as the xxii. personates Messiah in his state of humiliation; predicts the confusion of his enemies, his triumph, and the exultation of the faithful.

1 PLEAD Thou my cause, O Lord, my God,
 Fight Thou against my pow'rful foes;
Extend Thy shield, draw out Thy spear,
 And all their fierce assaults oppose.

2 Rise, great Jehovah, mighty Lord
 Guard me by Thine omnipotence;
Say to my soul, I am thy God,
 Thy strength, salvation, and defence.

3 All they, who hate Thy saints shall fall,
 Confounded by Thy potent word,
Driv'n like the chaff before the wind,
 Chas'd by the Angel of the Lord.

4 My soul shall triumph in Thy name,
 From ev'ry foe, from death set free;
My very bones shall praise, and say,
 Who, is a God O Lord, like Thee?

PSALM 36.

5 O shout for joy, ye saints of GOD,
   Who love MESSIAH's righteous cause:
Shew forth the honor of His name,
   Maintain His truth, revere His Laws.

6 The LORD of hosts be magnified,
   Who in His servants' bliss delights;
My tongue shall speak His righteousness,
   Whose mercy endless praise excites.

PSALM XXXVI. (L. M.)

The Prophet, lamenting the principles and conversation of the wicked, raiseth his thoughts to Heaven and celebrates the mercy of Jehovah.

1 MY heart, oppress'd with deep concern,
   Beholds the men, who truth despise,
Whose multiplied transgressions prove
   No fear of GOD before their eyes.

2 High as the heav'ns, Thy mercy shines;
   High as the clouds Thy faithfulness;
Firm as the mountains stands Thy truth,
   Deep as the seas Thy righteousness.

3 How excellent Thy mercy LORD!
   Parent of all, Thou bounteous King,
Children of men shall learn to trust
   Under the shadow of Thy wing.

4 Fed with abundance in Thy house,
   With joy divine their hearts shall glow;
While heav'nly pleasures they partake,
   Where streams of life perpetual flow.

5 Fountain of life, O where shall man
   True life obtain, where but in Thee?

PSALM 37.

Where else, O uncreated light,
   Truth in its own pure radiance see?

6 Preserve me from the snares of pride,
   Hold thou me up, my soul restore,
While workers of iniquity
   Inglorious fall to rise no more.

PSALM XXXVII. (S. M.)

Advice and consolation to the Church and people of God, oppressed and afflicted.

1 FRET not thy anxious heart,
   Nor sink thy spirits down;
Soon, like the grass before the scythe,
   Shall every foe be gone.

2 Put thou thy trust in GOD,
   Intent on doing good;
In heav'nly pastures thou shalt dwell,
   Sustain'd with living food.

3 Delight thou in the LORD,
   And to His glory live;
Then all the good thy heart desires
   GOD will most richly give.

4 To Him commit thy cause.
   Confide and mark His way;
Thy righteousness shall shine as light,
   Thy judgment clear as day,

5 The meek possess the earth,
   Their joys shall never cease;
Content and calm delight insures,
   Th' abundance of their peace.

PSALM 37.

6. Though little in this world
    The righteous may possess,
'Tis better far then Ophir's gold,
    For GOD their store doth bless.

PART II.

7 GOD sees the good man's ways,
    And in him takes delight;
E'en tho' he falls, he falls to rise,
    Strong in JEHOVAH's might,

8 As he, by mercy taught,
    Hath pitied the distress'd;
Thus mercy shall on him descend,
    And on his offspring rest.

9 From sin depart, do good,
    The Law of GOD adore;
Wait thou on Him, observe His way,
    And dwell for evermore.

10 Behold the upright man,
    In death his joys encrease;
While sinners fall, he soars to bliss,
    His end is perfect peace.

11 The LORD His people loves;
    They trust His sacred word,
Their refuge, strength, in all distress,
    SALVATION's of the LORD.

PSALM XXXVIII. *(L.M.)*

The third penitential Psalm, an act of deep humiliation and confession of sin.

1 O Lord, rebuke me not in wrath,
   Thy just displeasure, Lord, withdraw;
Thine arrows pierce my inmost soul,
   Oh, stay the terrors of Thy Law.

2 Bereft of peace and rest and hope,
   Guilt presseth down my wearied soul;
No hand but Thine can heal the wound,
   No grace but Thine my fears controul.

3 Bow'd down beneath th' oppressive load,
   Mourning I pass the wearied day;
My groanings are not hid from Thee,
   In mercy take my sins away.

4 My strength decays, my sight hath fail'd,
   Lord bid Thy just displeasure cease;
God of Salvation plead my cause,
   Thy grace alone restores my peace.

5 Forsake me not, O Lord my God,
   My foes repel, my sins subdue;
Thou art my hope, on Thee I wait,
   Thy mercy's great, Thy promise true.

PSALM XXXIX. *C.M.*

Appointed by the Church for a funeral Psalm, a meditation on the shortness of life, combined with faith, hope, and submission.

1 MY God, the transient life of man
   My pensive heart dismays;

PSALM 39.

The solemn truth restrains my tongue,
   And calls to mind my ways.

2 O what is life, a very span,
   If once compar'd to Thee!
Man in his best estate appears,
   But dust and vanity.

3 Teach me, O Lord, to know my end,
   The measure of my days,
Teach me to learn how frail I am,
   How soon my strength decays.

4 See, man in his vain shadow walk,
   Disquieted, in vain
He heaps up wealth, nor knows for whom,
   Blinded with sordid gain.

5 O Lord, my God, what wait I for?
   My hope I place in Thee;
My rock, my trust, in Thee alone,
   Substantial good I see.

6 Thy stroke my trembling spirit awes,
   Thy wisdom spake the word;
I'm dumb; I open not my mouth,
   The deed is of the Lord.

7 Yet may a sinner plead with God,
   Remove th' impending storm,
Nor let divine omnipotence,
   Consume a dying worm.

8 Spare me, O God, in mercy spare,
   Thy sojourner below.
And form my soul for better worlds,
   Before from hence I go.

PSALM XXXIX. II Metre. *(C. M.)*

1 GOD of my life, look gently down,
  Behold the pains I feel;
Lord, I am dumb before Thy throne,
  Nor dare dispute Thy will.

2 Diseases are Thy servants, Lord,
  They come at Thy command;
Be silent then each murmuring word,
  Against God's chastening hand.

3 Yet let me plead with humble cries,
  Remove Thy sharp rebukes,
My strength consumes, my spirit dies
  Through Thy repeated strokes.

4 Crush'd as a moth beneath Thy hand,
  We moulder down to dust,
Our feeble pow'r can not withstand,
  And all our beauty's lost.

5 I'm but a sojourner below,
  As all my fathers were,
O may I be prepared to go
  When I the summons hear.

6 But if my life be spared awhile,
  Before my last remove,
O make Thy praise my business still,
  And I'll proclaim Thy love.

PSALM XL. (L. M.)

A prophecy of the glory of Messiah, the inefficacy of the legal sacrifices, the deliverance of the Church, by the incarnation, resurrection and doctrine of our great Redeemer.

1 AWAKE my soul in sacred lays,
    Resound the great IMMANUEL's praise,
The Son of GOD, mysterious plan,
Descends to earth, the Son of man.

2 New songs of praise our lips employ,
Let the whole Church proclaim the joy,
From the dark caverns of the grave,
Glorious He rises, strong to save.

3 Blest man, who GOD his trust hath made,
Renouncing all created aid,
Who, who Thy wond'rous works can tell,
Godlike, divine, unsearchable?

4 The blood of thousand victims slain,
To expiate sin is all in vain,
Then cries the SAVIOUR, lo, I come,
Mine be the curse, the sinner's doom.

5 The Law of truth is in His heart;
Mercy and peace His lips impart;
And congregations great shall prove,
Salvation, righteousness, and love.

6 Behold the man;—He faints, He sighs,
For man's offences, bleeds and dies,
Our countless sins He deigns to bear,
And pains extreme his body tear.

7 Rejoice ye saints, His pow'r proclaim,
Let all His foes be put to shame;

Glory in Him, who lov'd and died,
And shout, the LORD be magnified!

8 LORD to our suff'rings condescend,
Thy poor and needy, LORD, defend,
In tender pity, bow thine ear,
And soon for all Thy saints appear.

PSALM XL. II Metre. 7, 7.

1 HOLY wonder, heav'nly grace,
Come inspire our humble lays,
While the SAVIOUR's love we sing,
Whence our hopes and comforts spring

2 Man involv'd in guilt and woe,
Touch'd His tender bosom so,
That, when justice death demands,
Forth the great Deliv'rer stands.

3 JESUS cries. " Thy mercy shew,
" Lo! I come, Thy will to do;
" I the sacrifice will be,
" Death shall plunge his dart in me."

4 Tho' the form of GOD He bore,
Great in glory, great in pow'r,
See Him in our flesh array'd,
Lower than His angels made.

PSALM XLI. S. M.

The blessedness of the merciful, an exercise of prayer and praise.

1 BLEST is the man, whose heart
With kind compassion glows;
Who the rich luxury enjoys,
Of healing others' woes.

PSALM 41.

2 The needy blest by him,
 His charities record;
His works of love, His pious zeal,
 God will himself reward.

3 When in affliction's path,
 The Lord will be his friend;
Preserve, and keep his soul alive,
 And full deliv'rance send.

4 In sickness, pain, or death,
 His comforts shall abound;
God smooths his bed, and gives him peace,
 While heav'nly joys abound.

5 On earth preserv'd and bless'd,
 God will enrich his days;
His enemies shall own His worth,
 His God have all the praise.

6 Bless'd be the Lord our God,
 Eternally the same;
World without end proclaim His love,
 Extol His holy name.

PSALM XLI. II Metre. (C. M.)

1 HAPPY the man whose tender care
 Relieves the poor distress'd;
When troubles compass him about
 The Lord shall give him rest.

2 The Lord his life, with blessings crown'd,
 In safety shall prolong;
And disappoint the will of those,
 Who seek to do him wrong.

3 If he in languishing estate,
 Oppress'd with sickness lie;

PSALM 42.

The LORD will easy make his bed,
   And inward strength supply.

4 Let therefore Israel's LORD and GOD,
   From age to age be bless'd;
And all the people's glad applause,
   With loud Amens express'd.

PSALM XLII.   (L. M.)

David, by Absaloms rebellion, driven from Jerusalem, describes in pathetic strains his despondency and hope.

1 AS pants the hart fatigued, distress'd,
   For cooling streams, with thirst oppres'd;
So pants my soul for Thine abode,
   For Thee, my GOD, the living GOD.

2 By day, by night, o'erwhelm'd with tears,
   My daily food, my anxious fears;
My enemies my soul dismay,
   ' And, where's thy GOD, insulting say.

3 Those past endearments I lament,
   With saints when to Thy courts I went,
Thy courts for sacred joy design'd,
   Where multitudes in praise combin'd.

4 Why then, my soul, Thy anxious fear?
   Why thus cast down in sad despair?
Hope still in GOD, and thou shalt raise
   Anthems of glory to His praise.

5 Deep calls to deep, the billows roll,
   Thy storms alarm, oppress my soul;
Help me my GOD, Thy pow'r to trace
   In past memorials of Thy grace.

PSALM 42.

Lo! a reviving beam appears,
  Thy loving kindness, quells my fears;
Thou, LORD, my sinking soul shalt raise
  And gloomy night shall hear Thy praise.

Then why, my soul, thy plaintive moan,
  Why thus disquieted, cast down?
Hope thou in GOD, soon shalt thou raise
  Anthems of glory to His praise.

PSALM XLII. II Metre. (C. M.

AS pants the hart for cooling streams,
  When heated in the chace;
So longs my soul, O GOD, for Thee,
  And Thy refreshing grace.

For Thee, my GOD, the living GOD,
  My thirsty soul doth pine;
O! when shall I behold Thy face,
  Thou Majesty divine!

May I advance with songs of praise,
  My solemn vows to pay;
And join the highly favor'd throng,
  Who keep the sacred day.

Why restless, why cast down, my soul?
  Hope still; and thou shalt sing
The praise of Him who is Thy GOD,
  Thy health's eternal spring.

PSALM XLIII. (L. M.)

The same subject continued.

1 JUDGE me, O God, and plead my cause,
   Deceitful men, insult Thy Laws;
God of my strength, O tell me why,
As one far off, to Thee I cry?

2 O send from heav'n Thy truth, Thy light,
And lead me forth, with radiance bright,
To Thy blest courts, to view Thy face,
Thy holy hill, Thy dwelling place.

2 Then to Thy altar I'll repair,
And bring my grateful off'rings there,
Thy praises shall my harp employ,
O God, my God, with sacred joy.

4 Then why art thou cast down my soul,
Let trust in God thy fears controul;
Him will I praise in His abode,
Health of my countenance, my God.

PSALM XLIV. (L. M.)

The Church, recounting the mercies of God to his Servants of old time, declares her confidence in his mercy, and implores divine help.

1 O God our help in days of old
   Our ancestors Thy acts have told,
Israel possessed the promis'd Land,
Victorious by Thy mighty hand.

2 Thou great Jehovah art our King,
Thy all triumphant pow'r we sing;

Psalm 45.

Nor bow, nor warlike sword we name,
Thine all the glory, Thine the fame.

4 But now Thy absence, Lord, we mourn,
Return, O God of hosts, return;
Behold our grief, Thy help we claim,
Reproach'd, afflicted, put to shame.

5 O hide not Thou Thy face, arise,
Nor yet Thy servant's cause despise;
Rise for our help, O Lord, awake,
d save us for Thy mercies sake.

Psalm XLV. (L. M.)

Appointed by the Church, for Christmas Day, as celebrating the Majesty and conquests of King Messiah, and the excellence and glory of the Church.

1 AWAKE, my heart, with joy record,
The brilliant triumphs of thy Lord.
My tongue, divinely influenc'd sing
Messiah's praise, th' eternal King.

2 O fairer than the sons of men!
Truth grace and mercy mark Thy reign;
Celestial joys Thy steps surround,
Of God with bliss eternal crown'd.

3 Gird on Thy sword, most mighty Prince,
Thy glorious majesty evince;
Truth, meekness, righteousness combine,
And round Thy car emblazon'd shine.

4 Ride on and conquer, mighty Lord,
Direct the arrows of Thy word;

Psalm 45.

Subdue Thy foes; Thy conquests spread
Triumphs of mercy crown Thy head.

5 Thy throne, O GOD, shall ever last,
Ages to come, from ages past;
The sceptre of Thy righteousness
All nations shall with justice bless.

6 Celestial grace Thy pow'r attends;
On Thee, the oil of joy descends;
The odours of Thy vestments rise,
And fill the palace of the skies;

7 Thou lovest truth, Thou HOLY ONE,
Grace, mercy, peace adorn Thy throne,
And GOD, thy GOD, to Thee hath giv'n,
The plenitude of joy in heav'n.

PART II.

8 At GOD's right hand the Church is seen,
Array'd in splendor stands the Queen,
Her vesture gold, her beauteous dress
The LORD her strength and righteousness.

9 Daughter of Salem, all within
Is glorious, purified and clean;
Garments of holiness are thine,
Mercy, and truth, and grace divine.

10 See sons and daughters yet unborn
Thy splendid retinue adorn;
By saints escorted, lo, they rise,
To swell Thy triumphs in the skies.

11 The heav'nly gates expand; they come
Triumphant to their glorious home,

Psalm 46.

The sacred mansion bought by blood
The palace of their Saviour God.

12 Heiress of glory, upward soar,
   Thy temp'ral state regard no more;
   So shall the King thy graces own,
   Adore and worship Him alone.

13 Let the whole world His praises sing;
   Let ev'ry age its tribute bring;
   Thy glorious name enroll'd shall shine,
   And praise, eternal praise, be Thine.

PSALM XLVL

The Church, in time of trouble, exults in the power, might and wonderful works of her victorious Lord.

1 GOD is our refuge and defence,
    Our present help, our confidence,
     When storms of woe assail.
  We will not fear, tho' tempests roar,
  Or scatter'd mountains strew the shore,
    Or boist'rous storms prevail.

2 There is a stream, whose gentler flow,
  Shall teach with gladden'd heart to glow
    The city of our God.
  See pow'r divine her fears expels;
  God in the midst of Zion dwells,
    And owns her His abode.

3 Let heathens rage, let kingdoms move,
  Jehovah thunders from above
    Earth melts and hears His voice.

Psalm 47.

The LORD of hosts is our defence;
Our refuge His omnipotence;
 In Jacob's GOD rejoice.

4 O come, behold the works of GOD,
The desolations of His rod,
 His awful pow'r adore;
Behold He reigns the Prince of Peace,
He breaks the bow, bids tumult cease,
 Nations learn war no more.

5 Be still, and bow before His throne,
Know He is GOD, He reigns alone,
 Exalted be His name;
On Him, the LORD of hosts, rely;
The GOD of Jacob rules the sky,
 O'er earth and heav'n, supreme.

PSALM XLVII. (C. M.)

Appointed by the Church for ascension Day, it celebrates the victories and triumph of Christ, the establishment of his kingdom, and the conversion of the Gentiles.

1 O All ye people anthems raise,
   With lifted hands rejoice
Triumphant in JEHOVAH's praise,
  Exult with joyful voice.

2 The LORD most high the nations rules
 From his exalted seat,
Our lot selects, the foe controuls
 Beneath our conq'ring feet.

3 GOD is gone up, the trumpets sound
 His glorious deeds on high,
Sing praises to our GOD, resound
 His praises thro' the sky.

Psalm 48.

5 God reigns the heathen world to bless
   To guide to endless day,
And on His throne of holiness,
   He rules with gentlest sway.

6 The Gentiles crowd to Thy abode
   And hail Thy sacred dome,
Kings, Princes worship Abraham's God,
   And heirs of bliss become.

PSALM XLVIII. I. Metre (L. M.)

The glory, privileges and stability of the Church.

1 GREAT is the Lord, His praise express,
   O Zion, city of our God,
Thou mountain of His holiness,
   Joy of the earth, the King's abode,

2 God in thy palaces is known,
   His people's refuge, and defence;
Kings of the earth His pow'r shall own,
   The arm of His omnipotence,

3 The saints of God oft heard and prov'd,
   As prophets sang in ages past,
The Church of God abides belov'd,
   And to eternity shall last.

4 Here may our souls in patience wait.
   Thy loving kindness to behold;
Lord, in Thy temple, at Thy gate,
   The mysteries of Thy grace unfold!

5 Great God, according to Thy name,
   Thy praise throughout the world extends;
Thy righteousness exalts Thy fame,
   Thy hand to succour man descends.

PSALM 48.

4 Daughter of Judah, then rejoice,
   Triumphant in Thy sov'reign LORD,
Behold His judgment, lift thy voice,
   Let age to age His truth record.

5 Walk about Zion, her abode,
   Her bulwarks, strength defence proclaim;
JEHOVAH ever is our GOD;
   Our guide thro' life, in death the same.

PSALM XLVIII. II Metre. (S. M.)

1 GREAT is the LORD our GOD,
   And let His praise be great,
He makes His churches His abode,
   His most delightful seat.

2 These temples of His grace,
   How beautiful they stand:
The honors of our native place,
   And bulwarks of our land.

3 Let strangers walk around
   The city where we dwell,
Compass and view Thine holy ground,
   And mark the building well.

4 The orders of Thy house,
   The worship of Thy court,
The chearful songs, the solemn vows,
   And make a fair report.

5 In Sion GOD is known,
   A refuge in distress;
How bright hath His salvation shone
   Through all her palaces!

6 In ev'ry new distress,
   We to Thy house repair;
We'll think upon Thy wond'rous grace,
   And seek deliv'rance there.

PSALM 49—50.

PSALM XLIX. (7,7.

The vanity of the world and prospects of the righteous.

1 HEARKEN, all mankind, give ear,
 Sons of men attentive hear;
 Hear true wisdom from on high,
 Learn to live, prepare to die.

2 Human means can not procure
 One short respite from the hour;
 Death advances, dust to dust
 Sinks the sinner and the just.

3 Seek not gold, nor fame, nor pow'r,
 Pageants of a transcient hour;
 Learn true happiness to prove,
 Set thy heart on joys above.

4 When the thoughtless sinner dies,
 Thou to realms of bliss shalt rise;
 God thy Spirit will receive,
 Rise victorious o'er the grave.

5 Raise my heart to joys untold,
 Glory brighter far than gold,
 Form my soul for Thine abode,
 There to dwell with Thee, my God.

PSALM L. Old 118th.

The Majesty of God, his awful judgment of the world and compassion to the righteous.

PSALM 51.

2 Our God shall come, at his stern bar,
 The world assembles from afar,
  God speaks; with solemn awe they hear.
 Hark, th' eternal Judge on high,
 Gather my saints, He saith, draw nigh,
  His voice dispels their ev'ry fear.

3 Hear, O my people, hear, attend;
 Know, I am God, thy God, thy friend,
  Pay me thy vows, present thy praise;
 Call on me in affliction's hour;
 I'll succour thee with mighty pow'r,
  And glorify my truth and grace.

4 Ye, who forget your God, give ear;
 Repentant turn, His vengeance fear,
  Consider and obey His word.
 His saints, who offer praise below,
 God will approve, confess and shew,
  The great salvation of the Lord.

PSALM LI. (L. M.)

1 SHEW pity Lord! O Lord, forgive,
 Let a repenting sinner live:
 Are not Thy mercies large and free?
 May not a sinner trust in Thee?

2 My sins are great, but don't surpass
 The pow'r and glory of Thy grace;
 Great God! Thy nature hath no bound,
 So let Thy pard'ning love be found.

3 O wash my soul from ev'ry stain,
 And make my guilty conscience clean
 Here on my heart the burden lies,
 And past offences pain mine eyes.

PSALM 57.

4 My lips with shame my sins confess,
  Against Thy Law, against Thy grace;
  LORD, should Thy judgment grow severe,
  I am condemn'd, but Thou art clear.

5 Yet save a trembling sinner, LORD,
  Whose hope still hov'ring round Thy word
  Would light on some sweet promise there,
  Some sure support against despair.

PSALM LVII.   (L. M.)

1 THY mercy, LORD, to me extend,
  On Thy protection I depend;
  For shelter to Thy wings I haste,
  Until the storm of life is past.

2 Be Thou, O GOD, exalted high;
  And as Thy glory fills the sky,
  So let it be on earth display'd
  Till Thou art here, as there obey'd.

3 O GOD my heart is fix'd, 'tis bent,
  Its thankful tribute to present;
  And with my heart, my voice I'll raise,
  To Thee, my GOD, in songs of praise.

4 Awake my glory; harp and lute,
  No longer let your strings be mute.
  And I, my tuneful part to take,
  Will with the early dawn awake.

5 Thy praises LORD, I will resound
  To all the list'ning nations round;
  Thy mercy highest heav'n transcends;
  Thy truth beyond the clouds extends.

Psalm 63.

6 Be Thou, O God, exalted high;
And as Thy glory fills the sky,
So let it be on earth display'd,
Till Thou art here, as there, obey'd.

PSALM LXIII. (Old 113th.)

1 O God, my gracious God, to Thee
My early prayers shall offer'd be;
For Thee my thirsty soul does pant;
My fainting strength implores Thy grace,
Within this dry, this barren place,
Where I refreshing waters want.

2 O to my longing eyes once more
That view of glorious pow'r restore,
Which Thy Majestic house displays,
Because to me Thy wond'rous love,
Than life itself does dearer prove,
My lips shall always speak Thy praise.

3 My life, while I that life enjoy,
In blessing God may I employ,
With lifted hands adore Thy name;
My soul's content shall be more great
Than their's, who dwell in earthly state,
While I with joy Thy praise proclaim.

4 When down I lie, sweet sleep to find,
Thou, Lord, art present to my mind;
And when I wake in dead of night;
Because Thou still dost succour bring
Beneath the shadow of Thy wing:
I rest with safety and delight.

Psalm 63.

I METRE. (L. M.)

1 O God my God! my all Thou art,
  E'er shines the dawn of rising day;
  Thy sov'reign light within my heart,
  Thine all enliv'ning pow'r display.

2 In a dry land, behold I place
  My whole desire on Thee my Lord,
  Yea, more I joy to gain Thy grace,
  Than all earth's treasure can afford!

3 O Lord, within Thy sacred gates,
  Where I so oft have sought for Thee;
  Again my longing spirit waits,
  That fulness of delight to see.

4 More dear than life itself, Thy love
  My heart and tongue shall still employ;
  Thy love to sing, Thy grace to prove,
  Be this my glory, peace and joy.

5 In blessing Thee with thankful songs,
  My happy life shall glide away:
  The praise that to Thy name belongs,
  Daily with lifted hands I pay.

6 Abundant sweetness! while I sing,
  Thy love my favor'd soul o'erflows;
  Secure in Thee my God, my King:
  Of glory that no period knows.

7 Beneath Thy smiles O may I live,
  By Thy right hand upheld and blest;
  Under the shadow of Thy wing,
  I trust, I wait, for endless rest.

PSALM 65.

PSALM LXV. (*L. M.*)

1 FOR Thee, O God, our constant praise
  In Zion waits, Thy chosen seat:
Our promis'd altars there we raise,
And all our zealous vows compleat.

2 O Thou, who to my humble prayer
Didst always lend a gracious ear,
To Thee shall all mankind repair,
And at Thy gracious throne appear.

3 Our sins, tho' numberless in vain
To stop Thy flowing mercy try;
Whilst Thou o'erlooks the guilty stain
And washest out the crimson dye.

4 Blest is the man who near Thee plac'd,
Within thy sacred dwelling lives;
Whilst we at humbler distance, taste
The vast delights Thy temple gives.

PART II. (*L. M.*)

1 GREAT GOD, from Thy exhaustless store
  Thy rain relieves the thirsty ground;
Makes lands, that barren were before,
With corn and useful fruits abound.

2 Thy goodness does the circling year
With fresh returns of plenty crown;
Where'er Thy glorious paths appear,
Thy fruitful clouds drop fatness down.

3 Large flocks with fleecy wool adorn
    The cheerful plains; the vallies bring
Their plenteous crops of full-ear'd corn,
    They seem for joy to shout and sing.

4 Thy works pronounce Thy pow'r divine;
    Thro' ev'ry month Thy gifts appear;
O'er ev'ry field Thy glories shine,
    Great GOD! Thy goodness crowns the year.

PSALM LXVII.   (S. M.)

1 TO bless Thy chosen race,
    In mercy, LORD, incline:
And cause the brightness of Thy face
    On all Thy saints to shine.

2 O let Thy wond'rous ways
    Through all the world be known;
Whilst distant lands their tribute pay,
    And Thy salvation own,

3 Let diff'ring nations join
    To celebrate Thy fame;
Let all the world, O LORD, combine
    To praise Thy glorious name.

4 O let them shout and sing,
    Dissolv'd in holy mirth:
For Thou, the righteous Judge and King,
    Dost govern all the earth.

5 Let diff'ring nations join
    To celebrate Thy fame:
Let all the world, O LORD, combine
    To praise Thy glorious name.

Psalm 68.

6 Then shall the teeming ground
  A large increase disclose:
And we with mercy shall be crown'd,
  Which God, our God, bestows.

7 Then God upon our land
  Shall constant blessings show'r,
And all the world in awe shall stand
  Of His resistless pow'r.

PSALM LXVIII. ver. 17 & 18.   (L. M.)

1 LORD, when Thou didst ascend on high
  Ten thousand angels fill'd the sky:
Those heav'nly guards around Thee wait
Like chariots that attend Thy state.

2 Not Sinai's mountain could appear
More glorious when the Lord was there;
While He pronounc'd His sacred law,
And struck the chosen tribes with awe.

3 How bright the triumph none can tell,
When the rebellious pow'rs of hell,
Who thousand souls had captives made,
Were all in chains like captives led.

4 Rais'd by Thy Father to Thy throne,
Thou sent'st the promis'd Spirit down,
With gifts and grace for rebel men,
That God might dwell on earth again.

5 Kingdoms and thrones to God belong;
Crown Him, ye nations, in your song:
His wond'rous names and pow'rs rehearse;
His honours shall enrich your verse.

Psalm 71.

6 By His right hand His saints shall rise,
From the deep earth or deeper seas;
He'll bring them to His courts above,
There shall they taste His special love.

PSALM LXXI. ver. 5—9,   (C. M.)

1 MY God, my everlasting hope,
   My trust is in Thy truth;
Thy hands have held my childhood up,
   And strengthen'd all my youth.

2 Still has my life new wonders seen
   Repeated ev'ry year:
Behold! my days, which yet remain,
   I trust them to Thy care.

3 Reject me not when strength declines,
   When hoary hairs arise;
And round me let Thy glory shine,
   Whene'er Thy servant dies.

4 Then, in the hist'ry of my age,
   When men review my days,
They'll read Thy love in ev'ry page,
   In ev'ry line Thy praise.

PART II, verse 15.   (C. M.)

1 MY Saviour, my Almighty Friend,
   When I begin Thy praise,
Where will the growing numbers end,
   The numbers of Thy grace?

2 Thou art my everlasting trust,
   Thy goodness I adore;

PSALM 72.

Teach Thou my heart, inspire my tongue,
  To praise Thee more and more.

3 My feet shall travel all the length
    Of the celestial road,
  And march with courage in Thy strength
    To see my LORD and GOD.

4 Thy mercy daily I'll proclaim,
    Thy great salvation own,
  The glories of Thy righteousness,
    And mention thine alone.

5 How will my lips rejoice to tell
    The vict'ries of my King!
  My soul redeem'd from death and hell,
    Shall Thy salvation sing.

6 Awake, awake my tuneful pow'rs;
    With this delightful song
  I'll entertain the darkest hours,
    Nor think the season long.

PSALM LXXII. (L. M.)

1 JESUS shall reign where'er the sun
    Doth His successive journies run;
  His kingdom stretch from shore to shore,
    'Till moons shall wax and wane no more.

2 To Him shall endless pray'r be made,
    And praises throng to crown His head:
  His name like sweet perfume shall rise
    With ev'ry morning sacrifice.

3 People and realms of ev'ry tongue
    Dwell on His love with sweetest song;

Psalm 76.

And infant voices shall proclaim
  Their early blessings on His name.

4 Blessings abound where'er he reigns;
  The pris'ner leaps to lose His chains;
The weary find eternal rest,
  And all the sons of want are blest.

5 Where He displays His healing pow'r,
  Death and the curse are known no more;
In Him the tribes of Adam boast
  More blessings than their father lost.

6 Let ev'ry creature rise and bring,
  Peculiar honours to their King;
Angels descend with songs again,
  And earth repeat the loud AMEN.

Psalm LXXVI. (II. Metre.)

1 IN Judah is JEHOVAH known,
    There His almighty deeds are shewn,
  His Name in Jacob does excel:
    His sanctuary in Salem stands;
  His majesty, which heav'n commands,
    In Sion condescends to dwell.

2 He brake the bow and arrow there,
    The sword, the battle, shield and spear,
  There slain the mighty armies lie;
    Let Sion's fame thro' earth be spread;
  Daughter of Salem lift Thy head:
    Re-sound Thy triumph thro' the sky.

3 Earth stood aghast, and heard her doom
    Array'd in judgment GOD did come,

Psalm 84.

The meek with justice to restore;
  The wrath of man shall yield Thee praise,
And all its fury only raise
  The triumphs of almighty pow'r.

4 Bring to the LORD, ye nations, bring
  Your off'rings to th' eternal King;
To His great name due homage pay:
  He proudest enemies can quell;
In Sion he will ever dwell;
  His praise exalt to endless day.

PSALM LXXXIV. (C. M.)

1 O GOD of hosts, the mighty LORD,
  How lovely is the place
Where Thou, enthron'd in glory, shew'st
  The brightness of Thy face!

2 My longing soul faints with desire
  To view Thy blest abode:
My panting heart and flesh cry out
  For Thee the living GOD.

3 O LORD of Hosts my King, my GOD,
  How highly blest are they,
Who in Thy temple always dwell,
  And there Thy praise display.

4 Thy saints advance from strength to strength,
  Approaching still more near;
'Till all on Sion's holy mount
  Before their GOD appear.

5 For GOD, who is our sun and shield,
  Will grace and glory give;
And no good thing will GOD withhold
  From those who justly live.

Psalm 84.

6 O God whom heav'nly hosts obey,
 How highly blest is he,
Whose hope, and trust, securely plac'd,
 Is still repos'd on Thee.

PSALM LXXXIV. III Metre. (*C. M.*)

1 MY soul, how lovely is the place
 To which thy God resorts!
'Tis heav'n to see His sacred face,
 Tho' in His earthly courts.

2 There the great Monarch of the skies
 His saving pow'r displays,
And light breaks in upon our eyes
 With kind and quick'ning rays.

3 With Thy rich gifts, O heav'nly Dove,
 Descend and fill the place,
While Christ reveals His wond'rous love
 And sheds abroad His grace.

4 Here, mighty God, Thy words declare,
 The secrets of Thy will;
And lo! we seek Thy mercy here,
 And sing Thy praises still.

5 My heart and flesh cry out for Thee,
 While far from Thine abode;
When shall I tread Thy courts, and see
 My Saviour and my God?

6 To sit one day beneath Thine eye,
 And hear Thy gracious voice,
Exceeds a whole eternity
 Employ'd in earthly joys.

Psalm 86 & 89.

PSALM LXXXVI. (C. M.)

1 TO my complaints, O Lord my God,
  Thy gracious ear incline;
Hear me, distrest and destitute
  Of all relief but Thine.

2 Thou Lord art good, supremely good,
  And ready to forgive;
Plenteous in mercy, to all those,
  Who on Thy mercy live.

3 Teach me Thy way, O Lord, that I
  May ne'er from truth depart;
To fear Thy awful sacred name,
  Unite and fix my heart.

4 Thee will I praise, O Lord my God,
  Praise Thee with heart sincere;
And to Thy everlasting name
  Eternal trophies rear.

5 Thy boundless mercy shewn to me
  Transcends my pow'r to tell;
For Thou hast oft redeem'd my soul
  From lowest depths of hell.

6 Do Thou Thy constant goodness, Lord,
  To my assistance bring;
Of patience, mercy, peace, and truth,
  Thou everlasting spring.

PSALM LXXXIX. (L. M.)

1 THY mercies, Lord, shall be my song,
  My song on them shall ever dwell,
To ages yet unborn my tongue
  Thy never failing truth shall tell.

Psalm 90.

2 Thy faithfulness Thou wilt maintain,
    Thy mercy shall for ever last;
Thy truth eternal shall remain,
    As heav'n shall stand for ever fast.

3 For Thy stupendous grace and love
    Both heav'n and earth just homage owe,
Let choirs of angels praise above;
    Let saints assembled praise below.

4 Happy, thrice happy, they who hear,
    Who know Thy Gospel's joyful sound;
Who in Thy sacred courts appear,
    With thy most glorious presence crown'd.

5 Fulness of joy Thy saints shall bless,
    Who on Thy sacred name rely;
Exalted in Thy righteousness,
    Shall they ascend and claim the sky.

6 Strong in Thy strength shall they advance,
    Their conquests from Thy grace shall spring,
The LORD of hosts is our defence,
    Our glory, shield, our GOD, our King.

7 Blessed for ever be our LORD!
    Ye saints His praise repeat again.
Let all your strains His love record,
    For evermore—AMEN—AMEN.

PSALM XC. *(C. M.)*

1 O GOD, our help in ages past,
    Our hope for years to come;
Our shelter from the stormy blast,
    And our eternal home.

PSALM 90 & 91.

2 Under the shadow of Thy throne
 Thy saints have dwelt secure:
Sufficient is Thy arm alone,
 And our defence is sure.

3 Before the hills in order stood,
 Or earth receiv'd its frame;
From everlasting Thou art GOD
 To endless years the same.

4 A thousand ages, in Thy sight,
 Are, like the evening, gone;
Short as the watch that ends the night,
 Before the rising sun.

5 O GOD our help in ages past,
 Our hope for years to come,
Be Thou our guide while life shall last,
 And our eternal home.

PSALM XCI. (P. M.)

1 HE that hath GOD his guardian made
 Shall under the Almighty shade
 Secure and unalarm'd abide.
Thus to my soul of Him I'll say,
He is my fortress and my stay,
 My GOD in whom I will confide.

2 His tender love and watchful care,
 Shall keep thee from the fowler's snare,
 From danger, woe and pestilence;
He over thee his wings shall spread,
And cover thy unguarded head;
 His truth shall be thy strong defence.

Psalm 92.

3 Because, with humble confidence,
   Thou mak'st the LORD thy sure defence,
      And on the HIGHEST dost rely;
   Therefore thy GOD will honor thee,
   Preserve, protect, and set thee free,
      And fix thy glorious rest on high.

4 The LORD will answer at thy call,
   And rescue thee when ills befal,
      And raise to honour and renown;
   His peace shall give thy soul content;
   And, when thy happy life is spent,
      Salvation shall thy prospect crown.

PSALM XCII.   (L. M.)

1 SWEET is the work, my GOD, my King,
   To praise Thy name, give thanks and sing,
   To shew Thy love by morning light,
   And talk of all Thy truth by night.

2 Sweet is the day of sacred rest,
   No mortal care shall seize my breast:
   O may my heart in tune be found,
   Like David's harp of solemn sound!

3 My heart shall triumph in the LORD,
   And bless his works, and bless his word;
   Thy works of grace how bright they shine!
   How deep Thy counsels! how divine!

4 O may I see, and hear, and know,
   All I desire or wish below;
   And ev'ry pow'r find sweet employ
   In CHRIST's eternal world of joy.

Psalm 92 & 93.

5 Within God's court the righteous stand,
 Supported by His guardian hand,
 Blest objects of his constant care,
 The bounties of His love they share.

6 Blest with Thy influence from above,
 They bear the fruits of faith and love;
 Time which doth all things else impair,
 Still makes them flourish strong and fair.

7 Laden with richest fruits they shew,
 Thou, Lord, art holy, just, and true;
 None who attend Thy gates shall find,
 A God unfaithful or unkind.

PSALM XCIII. *(L. M.)*

1 WITH glory clad, with strength array'd,
  The Lord, that o'er all nature reigns,
 The world's foundation strongly laid,
  And the vast fabric still sustains.

2 How surely 'stablish'd is Thy throne!
  Which shall no change or period see;
 For Thou, O Lord, and Thou alone,
  Art God from all eternity.

3 The floods, O Lord, lift up their voice,
  And toss the troubled waves on high
 But God above can still their noise,
  And make the angry sea comply.

4 Thy testimonies, Lord, are sure;
  Thy promises our fears dispel,
 O let Thy saints, in Thee secure,
  In truth and holiness excel.

Psalm 95.

PSALM XCV. (*L. M.*)

1 O COME, loud anthems let us sing,
   Loud thanks to our almighty King:
For we our voices high should raise,
When our salvation's Rock we praise.

2 Into His presence let us haste,
   To thank Him for His favours past;
To Him address, in joyful songs,
The praise that to His name belongs.

3 For GOD the LORD, enthron'd in state,
   Is with unrivall'd glory great;
A King superior far to all
Whom gods the heathens falsely call.

4 O let us to His courts repair,
   And bow with adoration there;
Down on our knees devoutly all
Before the LORD our Maker fall.

PSALM XCV. III Metre. (*S. M*)

1 COME, sound His praise abroad,
   And hymns of glory sing;
JEHOVAH is the sov'reign GOD,
   The universal King.

2 He form'd the deeps unknown;
   He gave the seas their bound,
The wat'ry worlds are all His own;
   And all the solid ground.

PSALM 97.

3 Come, worship at His throne,
  Come, bow before the LORD,
We are His works, and not our own,
  He form'd us by His word.

4 With humble souls adore,
  Come kneel before His face.
O may the creatures of His pow'r
  Be children of His grace.

PSALM XCVII. (L. M.)

1 HE reigns; the LORD, the Saviour reigns!
    Praise Him in high exalted strains;
  Let the whole earth in songs rejoice;
  Let distant islands join their voice.

2 Deep are His counsels and unknown:
  But grace and truth support His throne:
  Tho' gloomy clouds His way surround,
  Justice is their eternal ground.

3 In robes of judgment, lo! He comes,
  Shakes the wide earth, and cleaves the tombs;
  Before Him burns devouring fire,
  The mountains melt, the seas retire.

4 His enemies with sore dismay,
  Fly from the sight, and shun the day!
  Then lift your heads, ye saints, on high,
  And sing, for your redemption's nigh.

PSALM 93.

5 Immortal light and joys unknown,
Are for God's saints in darkness sown;
Those glorious seeds shall spring and rise,
And the bright harvest bless our eyes.

6 Rejoice, ye righteous, and record
The sacred honours of the Lord;
Proclaim the triumphs of His grace,
His justice, truth, and holiness.

PSALM XCVIII. (C. M.)

1 SING to the Lord a new-made song,
   Who wond'rous things hath done:
With His right hand, and holy arm
   The conquest He hath won.

2 The Lord, has thro'-th' astonish'd world
   Display'd His saving might,
And made His righteous acts appear
   In all the heathen's sight.

3 Of Is'rael's house His love and truth
   Have ever mindful been:
Wide earth's remotest parts the pow'r
   Of Israel's God have seen.

4 Rejoice, O world; the Lord is come!
   Let earth receive her King:
Let ev'ry heart prepare Him room,
   And all creation sing.

5 Rejoice, O earth, the Saviour reigns!
   Let men their songs employ;
Let fields and floods, rocks, hills, and plains
   Repeat the sounding joy.

Psalm 99.

6 No more let sins and sorrows grow,
   Nor thorns infest the ground;
He comes to make His blessings flow,
   Far as the curse is found.

7 He rules the world with truth and grace;
   And makes the nations prove
The glories of His righteousness,
   And wonders of His love.

Psalm XCIX. (S. M.)

1 THE God Jehovah reigns,
   Let all the nations fear:
Let sinners tremble at His throne,
   And saints be humble there.

2 Jesus the Saviour reigns,
   Let earth adore its Lord:
Bright cherubs His attendants stand,
   Swift to fulfil His word.

3 In Zion is His throne,
   His honours are divine;
His church shall make His wonders known,
   For there His glories shine.

4 How holy is His name?
   How terrible His praise!
Justice and truth, and judgment join
   In all His works of grace.

5 Exalt the Lord our God,
   And worship at His feet:
His nature is all holiness,
   And mercy is His seat.

PSALM 100.

PSALM C. *(L. M.)*
Old Version.

1 ALL people that on earth do dwell,
    Sing to the LORD with cheerful voice;
Him serve with fear, His praise forth-tell,
    Come ye before Him and rejoice.

2 The LORD, ye know, is GOD indeed,
    Without our aid He did us make;
We are His flock, He doth us feed,
    And for His sheep He doth us take.

3 O enter then His gates with praise,
    Approach with joy, His courts unto;
Praise, laud, and bless His name always,
    For it is seemly so to do.

4 For why? the LORD our GOD is good,
    His mercy is for ever sure:
His truth at all times firmly stood,
    And shall from age to age endure.

PSALM C. II Metre. *(L. M.)*

1 BEFORE Jehovah's awful throne,
    Ye nations bow with sacred joy;
Know that the LORD is GOD alone,
    He can create, and He destroy.

2 His sov'reign pow'r, without our aid,
Made us of clay, and form'd us men:
And when like wand'ring sheep we stray'd,
He brought us to His fold again.

3 We'll crowd Thy gates with thankful songs,
High as the heav'ns our voices raise;

Psalm 103.

And earth with her ten-thousand tongues,
Shall fill Thy courts with sounding praise.

2 Wide as the world is Thy command:
Vast as eternity Thy love;
Firm as a rock thy Truth must stand,
When rolling years shall cease to move.

Psalm CIII. (L. M.)

1 MY soul, inspir'd with sacred love,
  God's holy name for ever bless;
Of all his favors mindful prove,
  And still thy grateful thanks express.

2 'Tis God that all thy sins forgives,
  And after sickness makes thee sound;
From danger He thy life retrieves,
  By grace preserv'd, with mercy crown'd.

3 The Lord abounds with tender love,
  And unexampled acts of grace;
His waken'd wrath doth slowly move,
  His willing mercy flies apace.

4 God will not always harshly chide,
  But with His anger quickly parts
He loves His punishments to guide
  More by His love than our deserts.

5 As high as heav'n its arch extends
  Above this little spot of clay,
So much His boundless love transcends
  The small respects that we can pay.

6 As far as 'tis from East to West,
  So far has He our sins remov'd,

Psalm 103.

    Who with a father's tender breast
      Has such as fear him always lov'd.

7 The LORD, the universal King,
    In heav'n has fix'd His awful throne;
To Him, ye Angels, praises sing,
    In whose great strength His pow'r is shown.

8 Ye that His just commands obey,
    And hear and do His sacred will;
Ye hosts of His, this tribute pay,
    Who still what He ordains fulfil.

9 Let ev'ry creature jointly bless
    The mighty LORD: and thou my heart
With grateful joy thy thanks express,
    And in this concert bear thy part.

PSALM CIII. II. Metre. *(S. M.)*

1 MY soul repeat His praise,
    Whose mercies are so great,
Whose anger is so slow to rise,
    So ready to abate.

2 High as the heav'ns are rais'd
    Above the ground we tread,
So far the riches of His grace
    Our highest thoughts exceed.

3 The pity of the LORD,
    To those, who fear His name,
Is such as tender parents feel,
    He knows our feeble frame.

4 Our days are as the grass,
    Or like the morning flow'r:

Psalm 104—105.

If one sharp blast sweeps o'er the field,
  It withers in an hour.

5 But Thy compassions, Lord,
  To endless years endure;
And Children's Children ever find
  Thy word of promise sure.

PSALM CIV. *(L. M)*

1 BLESS God, my soul; Thou, Lord, alone
    Possessest empire without bounds:
  With honour Thou art crown'd, Thy throne
    Eternal majesty surrounds.

2 With light Thou dost Thyself enrobe,
    And glory for a garment take;
  Heav'ns curtains stretch beyond the globe
    Thy canopy of state to make.

3 In praising God while He prolongs
    My breath, I will that breath employ;
  And join devotion to my songs,
    Sincere, as in Him is my joy.

4 His glorious majesty adore;
    My soul praise thou His holy Name,
  Till with my song the list'ning world
    Join concert, and His praise proclaim.

PSALM CV. *(C. M.)*

1 O RENDER thanks, and bless the Lord,
    Invoke His sacred Name,
  Acquaint the nations with His deeds,
    His matchless deeds proclaim.

Psalm 106.

2 Sing to His praise in lofty hymns,
  His wond'rous works rehearse;
Make them the theme of your discourse,
  And subject of your verse.

3 Rejoice in His almighty Name,
  Alone to be ador'd;
And let their hearts o'erflow with joy,
  That humbly seek the Lord.

4 Seek ye the Lord, His saving strength,
  Devoutly still implore;
And, where He's ever present, seek
  His face for evermore.

5 His Cov'nant God has kept in mind,
  For num'rous ages past;
His Cov'nant, thousand ages more,
  Eternally shall last.

6 His statutes then may we observe,
  His sacred Laws obey;
For benefits so vast, may we
  Eternal praise display.

Psalm CVI. *(L. M.)*

1 O RENDER thanks to God above,
  The fountain of eternal love,
Whose mercy firm through ages past
Has stood, and shall for ever last.

2 Who can His mighty deeds express,
  Not only vast, but numberless?
What mortal eloquence can raise
His tribute of immortal praise?

Psalm 107.

3 Happy are they, and only they,
Who from Thy judgments fear to stray,
Who know what's right, not only so,
But aim to practise what they know.

4 Extend to me that favor, LORD,
Thou to Thy chosen dost afford;
When Thou return'st to set them free,
Let Thy salvation visit me.

4 O! may I worthy prove to see
Thy saints in full prosperity!
That I the joyful choir may join,
And count Thy people's triumph mine.

6 Let Israel's GOD be ever blest,
His name eternally confest;
Let all His saints with full accord,
Sing loud AMENS, Praise ye the Lord.

PSALM CVII. (L. M.

1 GIVE thanks to GOD: He reigns above,
Kind are His thoughts, His name is Love;
His mercy ages past have known,
And ages long to come shall own.

2 Let the redeemed of the LORD
The wonders of His grace record:
ISRAEL the nation whom He chose,
And rescued from their mighty foes.

3 In their distress to GOD they cried,
GOD was their SAVIOUR and their guide,
He led their march far wand'ring round;
'Twas the right path to Canaan's ground.

PSALM 107.

4 Thus when on heav'n we fix our eyes,
 And seek a rest above the skies;
 We have this desart world to pass,
 A long and dang'rous wilderness.

5 God feeds and clothes us all the way,
 He guides our footsteps lest we stray,
 He guards us with a pow'rful hand,
 And brings us to the heav'nly land.

6 O let the saints with joy record
 The truth and goodness of the LORD!
 How great His works! how kind His ways!
 Let ev'ry tongue pronounce His praise.

PSALM CVII. (C. M.)

1 HOW are Thy servants bless'd, O LORD!
 How sure is their defence!
 Eternal wisdom is their guide,
 Their help omnipotence.

2 In foreign realms, and lands remote,
 Supported by Thy care,
 Thro' burning climes they pass unhurt,
 And breathe in tainted air.

3 When by the dreadful tempest borne,
 High on the broken wave,
 They know Thou art not slow to hear,
 Nor impotent to save.

4 The storm is laid, the winds retire,
 Obedient to Thy will:
 The sea, that roars at Thy command,
 At Thy command is still.

Psalm 108.

5 Beset with dangers, fears, and deaths,
　　Thy goodness we'll adore,
　We'll praise Thee for Thy mercies past,
　　And humbly hope for more.

6 Our life, while Thou preserv'st that life,
　　Thy sacrifice shall be;
　And death, when death shall be our lot,
　　Shall join our souls to Thee.

Psalm CVIII. *(C. M.)*

1 O God, my heart is fully bent
　　To magnify Thy Name;
　My tongue with cheerful songs of praise
　　Shall celebrate Thy Fame.

2 Awake my lute; nor thou, my harp,
　　Thy warbling notes delay;
　Whilst I with early hymns of joy
　　Prevent the dawning day.

3 To all the list'ning tribes, O Lord,
　　Thy wonders I will tell,
　And to the nations sing Thy praise
　　That round about us dwell:

4 Because Thy mercy's boundless height
　　The highest Heav'n transcends,
　And far beyond th' aspiring clouds
　　Thy faithful Truth extends.

5 Be Thou, O God, exalted high
　　Above the starry frame;
　And let the world with one consent,
　　Confess Thy glorious name.

PSALM 110.

6 That all Thy chosen people Thee
   Their SAVIOUR may declare;
Let Thy right hand protect me still,
   And answer Thou my pray'r.

PSALM CX.   (C. M.)

1 TO CHRIST the LORD JEHOVAH spake,
   Enthron'd in glory sit,
At my right hand, till all Thy foes
   Shall fall beneath Thy feet.

2 JEHOVAH shall from Sion send
   The sceptre of His word;
That rod of strength, till all confess
   MESSIAH is the LORD.

3 The glorious day of pow'r appears,
   Day of victorious grace;
See willing nations crowd Thy courts
   In robes of holiness.

4 Behold the beauteous early dew,
   The spangles of the morn;
In countless myriads thus Thy saints
   Thy triumphs shall adorn.

5 The LORD hath sworn, nor will repent,
   In heav'n Thy high abode,
Eternal shall Thy priesthood last,
   Thou great high priest of GOD.

Psalm 110.

6 Conq'red by Thee, at Thy right hand,
   All enemies shall fall,
All Kings, all empires shall submit
   And own Thee, Lord of all.

7 But Thou must taste, it is decreed,
   Affliction in the way;
Perfect thro' suff'rings, glory crowns
   Thy head, in endless day.

PSALM CX. II Metre. (P. M.)

1 ALL hail, victorious Lord,
   At God's right hand above!
Triumphant o'er Thy foes!
   Triumphant in Thy love!
To Thee our joyful songs we bring;
To Thee we bow, all-conq'ring King!

2 O haste, victorious Prince,
   That happy glorious day,
When souls, like drops of dew,
   Shall own thy gentle sway:
O may it bless our longing eyes,
And bear our shouts beyond the skies.

3 All hail, exalted Priest!
   To Thee our all we give,
Enthron'd above the skies,
   All homage to receive!
There deign in our behalf to plead!
Yea, there for ever intercede.

4 God shall exalt thy head,
   And Thy high throne maintain:
In triumph Thou shalt lead,
   All who oppose Thy reign,
Thy foes beneath Thy feet shall lie
Prostrate to all eternity.

PSALM CXI.   (L. M.)

1 PRAISE ye the Lord; our God to praise
   My soul her utmost pow'rs shall raise;
With private friends, and in the throng
Of saints, His praise shall be my song.

2 His works for greatness though renown'd,
His wond'rous works with ease are found
By those, who seek for them aright,
And in the pious search delight.

3 His works are all of matchless fame,
And universal glory claim;
His truth confirm'd through ages past,
Shall to eternal ages last.

4 His bounty, like a flowing tide,
Has all His servants' wants supplied:
And He will ever keep in mind
His cov'nant with our fathers sign'd.

5 God sets His saints from bondage free,
And thus fulfils His grand decree,
For ever to remain the same;
Holy and rev'rend is His name.

Psalm 112.

6 Who Wisdom's sacred prize would win,
Must with the fear of God begin;
Immortal Praise and heav'nly skill
Have they, who know and do His will.

PSALM CXII. (L. M.)

1 THRICE happy man who fears the Lord,
Loves His commands, and trusts His word;
Honour and peace his days attend,
And blessings to his seed descend.

2 Compassion dwells upon his mind;
To works of mercy still inclin'd,
He lends the poor some present aid,
Or gives them, not to be repaid.

3 When times grow dark, and tidings spread
That fill his neighbours round with dread,
His heart is arm'd against the fear,
For God with all his pow'r is there.

4 His soul well fix'd upon the Lord,
Draws heav'nly courage from His word,
Amidst the darkness light shall rise,
To cheer his heart and bless his eyes.

5 He hath dispers'd his alms abroad,
His works are still before his God:
His hands, while they his alms bestow'd,
His glory's future harvest sow'd.

PSALM CXIII. (P. M.)

Appointed by the Church for Easter Day.

1 YE saints and servants of the Lord,
  The triumphs of His Name record,
    His sacred Name for ever bless;
  Where-e'er the circling sun displays
  His rising beams, or setting rays,
    Due praise to His great Name address.

2 God through the world extends His sway,
  The regions of eternal day
    But shadows of His glory are;
  With Him whose Majesty excels,
  Who made the heav'n in which He dwells,
    Let no created pow'r compare.

3 Though 'tis beneath His State to view
  In highest heav'n what Angels do,
    Yet He to Earth vouchsafes His care:
  The poor He raiseth from the dust,
  Exalting him amongst the just,
    The blessing of his grace to share.

4 O then His pow'r and grace declare,
  His love divine, His guardian care,
    Trust in His ever faithful word,
  Adore His everlasting fame,
  Extol the honours of his name,
    Who, who is like unto the Lord?

Psalm 116.

PSALM CXVI. (*C. M.*)

1 WHAT shall I render to my God,
    For all His kindness shown?
My feet shall visit Thine abode,
    My songs address Thy throne.

2 Among the saints that fill Thine house
    My off'rings shall be paid;
There shall my zeal perform the vows,
    My soul in anguish made.

3 How much is mercy Thy delight,
    Thou ever-blessed God!
How dear Thy servants in Thy sight!
    How precious is their blood!

4 How happy all Thy servants are!
    How great Thy grace to me!
My life, which Thou hast made Thy care,
    Lord, I devote to Thee.

5 Now I am thine, for ever Thine,
    Nor let my purpose move;
Thy hand has loos'd my bands of pain,
    And bound me with Thy love.

6 Here in Thy courts I pay my vow,
    And Thy rich grace record;
O all ye saints, who hear me now,
    Praise ye, O praise the Lord.

Psalm 117 & 118.

PSALM CXVII. *(L. M.)*

1 FROM all that dwell below the skies,
  Let the CREATOR's praise arise,
Let the REDEEMER's name be sung,
  Thro' ev'ry land by ev'ry tongue.

2 Eternal are Thy mercies, LORD;
  Eternal truth attends Thy word;
Thy praise shall sound from shore to shore,
  'Till suns shall rise and set no more.

PSALM CXVIII. *(C. M.)*

Appointed by the Church for Easter Day.

1 THIS is the day the LORD hath made,
  He calls the hours His own,
Let heav'n rejoice, let earth be glad,
  And praise surround the throne.

2 To-day CHRIST rose, and left the dead,
  And Satan's empire fell;
To-day the saints His triumphs spread,
  And all His wonders tell.

3 Hosanna to th' anointed King,
  To David's holy Son!
Help us, O Lord; descend and bring
  Salvation from Thy throne.

4 Blest be the LORD who comes to men
  With messages of grace;
To ransom by His bitter pain,
  And save the fallen race.

Psalm 121.

5 Hosanna in the highest strains
   The church on earth can raise;
The highest heav'ns in which He reigns,
   Shall give Him nobler praise.

PSALM CXXI. *(C. M.)*

1 TO Sion's hill I lift my eyes,
   From thence expecting aid;
From Sion's hill and Sion's God,
   Who heav'n and earth has made.

2 Then, O my soul, in safety rest,
   Thy Guardian will not sleep;
The mighty Lord, who Israel guards,
   With watchful care will keep.

3 Shelter'd beneath th' Almighty wings
   Thou shalt securely rest,
Where neither sun nor moon shall thee
   By day or night molest.

4 His constant care, throughout thy life,
   Shall guard from ev'ry ill;
In going out, in coming in,
   Thy Lord preserves thee still.

5 At home, abroad, in peace, in war,
   Thy God shall thee defend;
Conduct thee thro' life's pilgrimage
   Safe to thy journey's end.

Psalm 122.

6 Thus God His people ever guards
   From all impending harms;
And evermore around them spreads
   His everlasting arms.

Psalm CXXII. *(P. M.)*

1 THE joyful morn, my God is come,
   That calls me to Thy honor'd dome
    Thy presence to adore,
My feet the summons shall attend
With willing steps thy courts ascend,
    And tread the hallow'd floor.

2 Hither from earth's remotest end,
Lo, the redeem'd of God ascend,
    Their offerings hither bring,
Here crown'd with everlasting joy
In hymns of praise their tongues employ,
    And hail th' immortal King.

3 Behold, to our expecting eyes
Fair Sion's towers in prospect rise;
    E'en now, with glad survey,
Behold her mansions, that contain
Angelic forms, a splendid train,
    Who shine in endless day.

4 Let me, blest seat, my name behold
Among thy Citizens enroll'd,
    In Thee for ever dwell,

Psalm 125.

Let faith and hope my steps attend,
Be grace divine my constant friend,
  And bid the world farewel.

5 Seat[...]y friends and brethren hail!
Ne'er let my tongue, O Sion, fail
  To bless Thy lov'd abode!
Ne'er cease the zeal that in me glows,
Thy good to seek, whose walls enclose
  The mansions of my God.

PSALM CXXV. (C. M.)

1 WHO in the Lord Jehovah trust,
    Shall as mount Sion stand,
  Firm and immoveable be fix'd,
    By God's almighty hand.

2 Mark how the hills on every side
    Jerusalem inclose;
  So stands the Lord around His saints
    To guard them from their foes.

3 Secure in God's almighty name
    Let thy sure trust remain;
  God to His people will do good,
    Nor shall they trust in vain.

4 While all, who turn aside from Him,
    The Lord will soon destroy;
  He loves the just, and crowns his saints
    With endless peace and joy.

PSALM 126 & 130.

PSALM CXXVI. *(P. M.)*

1 THE heathen lands were forced to own,
That God a wond'rous work had done;
When Israel was set free.
" Redemption Thou hast wrought," we said,
Whereof our grateful hearts are glad;
We give the praise to Thee.

2 Now send, O send Thy powerful word,
To loose our fetter'd spirits, Lord;
We mourn a bondage still:
By sin to earth and death enslav'd,
When, Lord, from these shall we be sav'd
And full deliv'rance feel?

3 Turn then this worst captivity!
The mighty change belongs to Thee,
Our efforts all are vain;
Turn as the southern streams each heart,
From sin to Thee, nor let them start,
From Thee to sin again.

4 Who wait Thy time, although they sow
In tears, shall reap in joy, we know;
Their sin shall be forgiv'n;
Who weeps the penitential tear,
Bearing good seed, with joy shall bear
His fruitful sheaves to heav'n.

PSALM CXXX. *(C. M.)*

OUT of the depth of self-despair,
Help us, O Lord, to cry;

Psalm 132.

  Our misery mark, attend our prayer,
    And bring salvation nigh.

2 If Thou art rig'rously severe,
    Who may the test abide!
  O where shall sinful man appear
    Or how be justified!

3 But O! forgiveness is with Thee,
    That sinners may adore,
  With filial fear Thy goodness see,
    And never grieve Thee more.

4 Wait then my soul, confide in God,
    Mercy with Him remains;
  Plenteous Redemption bought with blood,
    To wash out all our stains.

5 His people God himself shall clear,
    Let Israel hope in Him;
  He will give strength and righteousness,
    And from all sin redeem.

PSAL CXXXII. (*L. M.*)

1 ARISE, O King of grace arise
    And enter to Thy rest!
  Lo! Thy Church waits with longing eyes,
    Thus to be own'd and blest.

2 Enter with all Thy glorious train,
    Thy Spirit and Thy word;
  All that the ark did once contain
    Could no such grace afford.

Psalm 133—134.

3 Here, mighty God! accept our vows,
  Here let Thy praise be spread;
Bless the provisions of Thy house,
  And fill Thy poor with bread.

4 Here let the Son of David reign,
  Let God's Anointed shine;
Justice and truth His court maintain,
  With love and pow'r divine.

5 Here let Him hold a lasting throne,
  And as His kingdom grows,
Fresh honor shall adorn His crown,
  And shame confound His foes.

Psalm CXXXIII. (P. M.)

1 HOW blest the sight, the joy how sweet,
  When brethren join'd with brethren meet
    In bands of mutual love!
  Less sweet the liquid fragrance, shed
  On Aaron's consecrated head,
    Distilling from above.

2 Less sweet the perfumes of his vest:
  Less sweet the dews on Hermon's breast,
    Or Sion's hill descend;
  The hill, which God with blessings crown'd,
  And promis'd grace, which knows no bound,
    And life that knows no end.

Psalm CXXXIV. - (C. M.)

1 BLESS God, ye servants that attend
    Upon His solemn state,
  That in His temple, night by night,
    With humble rev'rence wait:

2 Within His house lift up your hands,
    And bless His holy name;

From Sion bless Thy Israel, Lord,
  Who earth and heav'n didst frame.

PSALM CXXXV. (C. M.)

1 O Praise the Lord with one consent,
    And magnify His name;
  Let all the servants of the Lord
    His worthy praise proclaim.

2 Praise Him all ye that in His house
    Attend with constant care;
  Praise Him, and to His sacred Courts
    With humble zeal repair

3 For this our truest interest is,
    Glad hymns of praise to sing;
  And with loud songs to bless His Name,
    A most delightful thing.

4 For God His own peculiar choice
    The sons of Jacob makes;
  And Israel's offspring for His own
    Most valued treasure takes.

5 That God is great we often have
    By glad experience found;
  And oft have seen His wond'rous pow'r
    Above all glory crown'd.

6 Let all with thanks His wond'rous works
    In Sion's court proclaim;
  Let all in Salem, where He dwells,
    Exalt His holy Name.

PSALM CXXXVI. (L. M.)

1 GIVE to our God immortal praise!
    Mercy and truth are all his ways!
  Wonders of grace to God belong,
  Repeat His mercies in your song.

2 Give to the LORD of lords renown,
　The King of kings with glory crown;
　His mercies ever shall endure,
　When lords and kings are known no more.

3 He built the earth, He spread the sky,
　And fix'd the starry lights on high;
　Wonders of grace to GOD belong,
　Repeat His mercies in your song.

4 He fills the sun with morning light,
　He bids the moon direct the night;
　His mercies ever shall endure,
　When suns and moons shall shine no more.

5 GOD sent His Son with power to save
　From guilt, and darkness, and the grave;
　Wonders of grace to GOD belong,
　Repeat His mercies in your song.

6 Thro' this vain world He guides our feet,
　And leads us to His heav'nly seat;
　His mercies ever shall endure,
　When this vain world shall be no more.

PSALM CXXXVIII. (L. M.)

1 WITH all my powers of heart and tongue
　　I'll bless my Maker in my song;
　Angels shall hear the notes I raise,
　Approve the song, and join the praise.

2 Angels, that make Thy church their care,
　Shall witness my devotion there;
　While holy zeal directs my eyes
　To Thy fair temple in the skies.

3 I'll sing Thy truth and mercy, Lord;
　I'll sing the wonders of Thy word;
　Not all Thy works and name below,
　So much Thy power and glory shew.

PSALM 139.

4 To God I cried when trouble rose;
He heard me, and subdued my foes;
He did my rising fears controul,
And strength diffus'd thro' all my soul.

5 Amidst a thousand snares I stand,
Upheld and guarded by Thy hand,
Thy words my fainting soul revive,
And keep my dying faith alive.

6 Grace will compleat what grace begins,
To save from sorrow or from sins:
The work that wisdom undertakes,
Eternal mercy ne'er forsakes.

PSALM CXXXIX. *(L. M.)*

1 THOU, Lord, by strictest search hast known
My rising up and lying down;
My secret thoughts are known to Thee,
Known long before conceiv'd by me.

2 Thine eye my bed and path surveys,
Thine eye observeth all my ways;
Thou know'st the words I mean to speak,
Ere from my op'ning lips they break.

3 Surrounded by Thy pow'r I stand,
On ev'ry side I find Thy hand.
O skill, for human reach too high!
Too dazzling bright for mortal eye!

4 Where, Lord, could I Thy influence shun?
Or whither from Thy presence run?
Awake, asleep, at home, abroad,
I am surrounded still with God.

5 I'll praise Thee from whose hands I came,
A work of such a curious frame;
The wonders Thou in me hast shown,
My soul with grateful joy shall own.

6 Thy thoughts of love to me surmount
   The pow'r of numbers to recount,
   Far sooner could I reckon o'er
   The sands upon the ocean's shore.

7 O may I feel these truths imprest,
   Fix'd on my heart, whene'er I rest;
   And when I wake, each morning find
   GOD and His love possess my mind.

8 Try me, O GOD, O search my heart,
   And bid all evil thence depart.
   O guide me in Thy perfect way,
   To realms of everlasting day.

PSALM CXLII. *(S. M.)*

1 TO GOD with mournful voice
      In deep distress I pray'd;
   Made Him the umpire of my cause,
      My wrongs before Him laid.

2 I look'd, but found no friend
      To own me in distress;
   All refuge fail'd, and no man came,
      To pity or redress.

3 To Thee, my GOD, I pray'd
      Thou, LORD, my refuge art,
   My portion in the land of life
      Till life itself depart.

4 That I may praise Thy name,
      Help to Thy servant bring;
   And of Thy kind regard to me
      Assembled saints shall sing.

PSALM CXLV. *(C. M.*

1 THEE I will bless, my GOD and King.
      Thy endless praise proclaim:

Psalm 145.

This tribute daily I will bring,
  And ever bless Thy name.

2 Thou, Lord, beyond compare art great,
  And highly to be prais'd;
Thy Majesty, with boundless height,
  Above our knowledge rais'd.

3 Whilst I Thy glory and renown,
  And wond'rous works express,
The world with me Thy might shall own,
  And Thy great pow'r confess.

4 The praise that to Thy love belongs,
  They shall with joy proclaim;
Thy truth of all their grateful songs
  Shall be the constant Theme.

5 The Lord is good; fresh acts of grace
  His pity still supplies;
His anger moves with slowest pace,
  His willing mercy flies.

6 Thy love through earth extends its fame,
  By all Thy works exprest;
These shew Thy praise, and be Thy name
  For Ever, Ever, blest.

PART II. (C. M.)

1 SWEET is the mem'ry of Thy grace,
  My God, my heav'nly King,
Let age to age Thy righteousness
  In sounds of glory sing.

2 God reigns on high, but not confines
  His goodness to the skies,
Thro' the whole earth His bounty shines,
  And every want supplies.

Psalm 146.

3 With longing eyes Thy creatures wait
   On Thee, for daily food;
Thy lib'ral hand provides them meat,
   And fills their mouths with good.

4 How kind are Thy compassions, Lord!
   How slow Thine anger moves!
How soon He sends His pard'ning word
   To cheer the soul He loves.

5 Creatures, with all their endless race,
   Thy pow'r and praise proclaim:
May we who taste Thy richest grace,
   Delight to bless Thy name!

Psalm CXLVI. (C. M.)

1 O PRAISE the Lord, and thou, my soul,
   For ever bless His name:
His wond'rous love, while life shall last,
   My constant praise shall claim.

2 O happy he, who Jacob's God
   For his Protector takes;
Who still, with well-plac'd hope, the Lord
   His constant refuge makes.

3 The Lord who made both heav'n and earth,
   And all that they contain,
Will never quit His stedfast truth,
   Nor make His promise vain.

4 The poor opprest, from all their wrongs
   Are eas'd by His decree;
He gives the hungry needful food,
   And sets the pris'ners free.

5 By Him the blind receive their sight,
   The weak and fall'n He rears;
With kind regard and tender love
   He for the righteous cares.

Psalm 147.

6 The strangers He preserves from harm,
  The orphan kindly treats,
Defends the widow, and the wiles
  Of all their foes defeats.

7 How holy is the Lord, how just,
  How righteous all His ways!
How nigh to him, who with firm trust
  For His assistance prays!

8 The Lord thy God, O Sion, lives
  Thy everlasting King,
From age to age His reign endures:
  Let all His praises sing.

Psalm CXLVII. (L. M.)

1 PRAISE ye the Lord: 'tis good to raise
   Our hearts and voices in His praise,
His nature and His works invite
To make this duty our delight.

2 He form'd the stars, those heav'nly flames;
He counts their numbers, calls their names;
His wisdom's vast, and knows no bound,
A deep where all our thoughts are drown'd.

3 Great is our Lord, and great His might;
And all His glories infinite;
He crowns the meek, rewards the just,
And treads the wicked to the dust.

4 Sing to the Lord, exalt Him high,
Who spreads His clouds all round the sky;
There He prepares the fruitful rain,
Nor lets the drops descend in vain.

5 He makes the grass the hills adorn;
He clothes the smiling fields with corn,
The beasts with food His hands supply,
And the young ravens when they cry.

Psalm 148.

6 But saints are lovely in His sight;
   He views His children with delight;
   He sees their hope, he knows their fear,
   And looks and loves His image there.

7 Praise God from whom all blessings flow!
   Praise Him all creatures here below:
   Praise Him above ye heav'nly host:
   Praise Father, Son, and Holy Ghost.

PSALM CXLVIII. *(C. M.)*

1 PRAISE ye the Lord, immortal choir,
    Who fill the realms above,
  Praise Him who form'd you of His fire,
    Who feeds you with His love:
  Shine to His praise, ye crystal skies,
    The floor of His abode,
  Or veil in shades your thousand eyes
    Before your brighter God.

2 Thunder and hail, and fire and storms,
    The troops of His command,
  Appear in all your dreadful forms,
    And speak His awful hand:
  Shout to the Lord, ye surging seas,
    In your Majestic roar;
  Let wave to wave resound His praise,
    And shore reply to shore.

3 Wave your tall heads, ye lofty pines,
    To Him that bids you grow;
  Sweet clusters bend the fruitful vines
    On ev'ry thankful bough:
  Thus while the meaner creatures sing,
    Ye mortals, take the sound;
  Echo the glories of your King,
    Thro' all the nations round.

4 Praise ye the LORD, ye saints below,
    Brought nigh thro' Jesu's blood,
With praise seraphic ever glow
    And chaunt the love of GOD:
Praise Him in all the highest strains,
    Your noblest pow'rs afford.
While saints from yon celestial plains,
    Reply PRAISE YE THE LORD.

PSALM CXLVIII. P. M. III. Metre.

1 BEGIN, my soul, th' exalted lay,
    Let each enraptur'd thought obey,
      And praise th' Almighty's name:
Lo! heav'n and earth, and seas and skies,
In one melodious concert rise,
    To swell th' inspiring theme.

2 Angels, archangels swell the sound:
    Let all th' adoring thrones around
      GOD's boundless mercy sing;
Let ev'ry perfect saint above
Wake all the harmony of love,
    And touch the sweetest string.

3 Let Man, by purest motives sway'd,
    Join ev'ry pow'r the theme to spread,
      Let praise those pow'rs employ:
Chaunt His majestic Name around,
Till heav'n shall echo back the sound,
    The gen'ral theme of joy.

4 O praise Him, all beneath above,
   O praise Him, praise the GOD of love;
      Let ev'ry youth conspire,
Let age take up the tuneful lay,
Sigh His blest name, then soar away
    And praise with angels' lyre.

PSALM 149—150.

PSALM CXLIX. (*Old 104th.*)

1 O PRAISE ye the LORD, prepare your glad voice,
    His praise in the great assembly to sing;
In GOD our Creator let Israel rejoice;
    And children of Sion be glad in their King.

2 Exalt His great name, extol in your songs,
    Hosanna's combine his praise to express.
Our GOD taketh pleasure his saints to advance,
    And with His salvation the humble to bless.

3 With glory adorn'd his people shall sing,
    And perfect in bliss, His praises proclaim;
Such honor and triumph His saints shall enjoy,
    For ever and ever exalting His Name.

Gloria Patri.

By angels in heav'n of ev'ry degree,
And saints upon earth, all praise be address'd,
To GOD, Three in person, one GOD, ever blest,
As it has been, now is, and always shall be.

PSALM CL. (*P. M.*)

1 PRAISE the LORD, who reigns above,
    And keeps His courts below,
Praise the holy GOD of love,
    And all His greatness show,
Praise Him for His noble deeds,
    Praise Him for His matchless pow'r;
Him from whom all good proceeds,
    Let heav'n and earth adore.

2 Publish, spread to all around,
    The great IMMANUEL's name;

Psalm 150.

Let the trumpet's martial sound
 Him Lord of hosts proclaim;
Praise Him, ev'ry tuneful string,
 All the pow'rs of heav'nly art:
All the aids of music bring;
 The music of the heart.

3 Him, in whom they move and live,
 Let ev'ry creature sing;
Glory to their Maker give,
 And homage to their King:
Hallow'd be His name beneath,
 As in heav'n, on earth ador'd!
Praise the Lord, in ev'ry breath,
LET ALL THINGS PRAISE THE LORD.

MORNING HYMN.

151

By Bishop Kenn.   *L. M.*

1 AWAKE, my soul, and with the sun
   Thy daily stage of duty run:
   Shake off dull sloth and early rise
   To pay thy morning sacrifice.

2 Redeem thy mis-spent time that's past;
   Live this day, as if 'twere thy last
   T'improve thy talents take due care,
   For the great day thyself prepare.

3 Let all thy converse be sincere;
   Thy conscience as the noon-day clear;
   Think how th' all-seeing GOD thy ways
   And all thy secret thoughts surveys.

4 Wake and lift up thyself, my heart,
   And with the angels bear thy part;
   Who all night long unwearied sing,
   Glory to the eternal King.

5 Glory to Thee, who safe hast kept,
   And hast refresh'd me while I slept:
   Grant LORD, when I from death awake,
   I may of endless life partake.

6 Lord, I my vows to Thee renew;
Scatter my sins as morning dew;
Guard my first spring of thought and will,
And with Thy grace my spirit fill.

7 Direct, controul, suggest this day,
All I design to do, or say;
That all my pow'rs with all their might,
In thy sole glory may unite.

8 Praise God, from whom all blessings flow;
Praise Him, all creatures here below:
Praise Him above, ye heav'nly host:
Praise Father, Son, and Holy Ghost.

152

By Bishop Kenn.

Evening. L. M.

1 GLORY to Thee, my God, this night,
For all the blessings of the light,
Keep me, O keep me, King of kings,
Under Thy own Almighty wings.

2 Forgive me Lord, thro' Christ Thy Son,
The ills that I this day have done;
That with the world, myself and Thee,
I, ere I sleep, at peace may be.

3 Teach me to live, that I may dread,
The grave as little as my bed!
Teach me to die, that so I may
Triumphant rise, at the last day.

4 O may my soul on Thee repose;
And with sweet sleep mine eye lids close:
Sleep that may me more vig'rous make,
To serve my GOD, when I awake.

5 Praise GOD, from whom all blessings flow, &c.

PART II. 153

BY BISHOP KENN.   L. M.

1 BLESS'D angels, while we silent lie,
Your hallelujahs sing on high;
You joyful chaunt the EVER BLEST,
Before the throne, and never rest.

2 I with your choir celestial join
In offering up a hymn divine;
With you in heaven I hope to dwell,
And bid the night and world farewell.

3 O may I always ready stand,
With my lamp burning in my hand!
May I in sight of heav'n rejoice
Whene'er I hear my SAVIOUR's voice.

4 The sun in its meridian height
Is very darkness in Thy sight:
My soul O lighten and inflame
With thoughts and love of Thy great name!

5 Praise GOD, &c.

154

Morning   C. M.

1 LORD! for the mercies of the night,
    My humble thanks I pay,
Lord! now to Thee I dedicate,
    The first fruits of the day.

2 May this day praise Thee, O my God!
    And so may all my days;
And, O! may my eternal day,
    Be Thy eternal praise.

155

Evening   C. M.

1 NOW from the altar of my heart
    Let incense flames arise,
Assist me Lord to offer up
    My evening sacrifice.

2 Minutes and mercies multiplied
    Have made up all this day;
Minutes came quick, but mercies were
    More fleet, more free than they.

3 Lord of my time, whose hand hath set
    New time upon my score;
Thee may I praise for all my time—
    When time shall be no more.

156

THE LORD'S PRAYER.   P. M.

1 FATHER of all, eternal mind,
    In uncreated light enshrin'd
    Immensely good and great;

Thy children form'd and blest by Thee,
With filial love and homage, we
  Fall prostrate at Thy feet.

2 Thy name in hallow'd strains be sung,
Let ev'ry heart and ev'ry tongue
  The solemn concert join;
In loving, serving praising Thee
We find our chief felicity,
  But cannot add to Thine.

3 Thy righteous, mild, and sov'reign reign,
Throughout creation's ample plain,
  Let ev'ry being own:
LORD, in our hearts, where passions rude
With fierce tumultuous rage intrude,
  Erect Thy peaceful throne.

4 As angels round Thy seat above,
With joyful haste, and ardent love,
  Thy blest commands fulfil;
So let Thy creatures here below,
As far as thou hast giv'n to know,
  Perform Thy sacred will.

5 On Thee we day by day depend,
Our being's Author, and its end,
  Our daily wants supply;
With healthful meat our bodies feed,
Our souls sustain with living bread,
  Our souls that never die.

6 Extend Thy grace to ev'ry fault,
Each single action, word, and thought,

O let Thy love forgive!
For Thou hast taught our hearts to show
Divine forgiveness to our foe,
  Nor let resentment live.

7 Where tempting snares bestrew the way,
To lead unwary minds astray,
  Permit us not to tread;
Unless Thy gracious aid appear.
T'avert the threat'ning evil near,
  From our unguarded head.

8 Thy sacred Name we thus adore;
And thus Thy choicest gifts implore
  With joyful humble mind;
Because Thy pow'r and glory prove
Thy kingdom built on wisdom, love,
  Unceasing, unconfin'd. —

    VENITE, vide Psalm xcv.

157

TE DEUM LAUDAMUS.   *L. M.*

1 THEE sov'reign GOD! our anthems praise,
  We own Thee LORD in all Thy ways,
Thee, holy FATHER, earth's whole frame,
And heav'n's high powers e'er proclaim.

2 O HOLY, HOLY, HOLY, LORD!
Great GOD of Sabbath, they record
With splendor of Thy glory spread,
Is heav'n and earth replenished.

3 Thy praises fill the apostles' choir;
 The prophets in Thy praise conspire:
 Legions of martyrs swell the theme,
 And vocal blood resounds Thy name.

4 O GOD! Thy holy church to Thee
 Ascribe infinite majesty,
 Thy HOLY SPIRIT and Thy SON,
 The sacred THREE in Godhead ONE.

5 O King of glory, CHRIST most high!
 Thou co-eternal DEITY!
 Who, to save sinners from their doom,
 Didst not abhor the virgin's womb.

6 We sing Thy conquests o'er the grave!
 Aloud we sing Thy power to save!
 The realms of bliss we joyful see
 For all believers bought by Thee.

7 At GOD's right hand enthron'd on high,
 In all the glories of the sky,
 Till Thou in judgment shalt appear
 We hail Thee, and adore Thee there.

8 LORD of the living and the dead!
 O spare the souls for whom Thou bled;
 Unite us with Thy saints above,
 Their partners in a SAVIOUR's love.

9 O bless Thy heritage, defend,
 And keep us faithful to the end;
 Raise Thou our hearts, direct our way
 To magnify Thee day by day.

10 Our suppliant pray'r, O Lord, receive!
Father, Thy mercies ceaseless give,
And ever with us Lord be near,
Till we in glory shall appear.

158

BENEDICITE   P. M.

1 YE works of God, on Him alone,
In earth His foot-stool, heav'n His throne,
Be all your praise bestow'd;
Whose hand the beauteous fabrick made,
Whose eye the finish'd work survey'd,
And saw that all was good.

2 Ye angels, who with loud acclaim,
Admiring view'd the new born frame
And hail'd the eternal King;
Again proclaim your Maker's praise,
Again your thankful voices raise,
And touch the tuneful string.

Let all who vital breath enjoy,
Their ev'ry faculty employ,
Proclaim His praise divine;
Fire, air, and earth, and seas, and skies,
In one melodious concert rise,
And in full chorus join.

4 Ye thrones, dominions, virtues, pow'rs,
Combine your joyt songs with ours,
With us your voices raise;

From age to age extend the lay,
To heav'ns eternal Monarch pay
   Hymns of eternal praise.

5 Ye Priests of God the lay prolong,
Ye saints, exalt the grateful song
   To heav'ns eternal throne;
Till wonder seize the angelic train,
Pleas'd while they hear a mortal strain,
   So sweet, so like their own.

6 Ye spirits of the just and good,
Who eager for the blest abode,
   To heav'nly mansions soar;
O let your songs His praise display,
'Till heav'n itself shall melt away,
   And time shall be no more.

7 Praise Him, ye meek and humble train,
Ye saints, whom His decrees ordain
   The boundless bliss to share;
O! praise Him, 'till you take your way
To regions of eternal day,
   And reign for ever there.

8 Praise God who, reigns enthron'd on high,
Praise God the Son, who deign'd to die;
   The Holy Spirit praise.
Join the blest theme, angelic host,
Praise Father, Son and Holy Ghost,
   One glorious Anthem raise.

BENEDICTUS. Luke i, 68. *C. M.*

BY BISHOP PATRICK.

1 BLEST be the God of Israel,
His name be ever blest,
Who came from heav'n to visit us,
And all our bonds releas'd.

2 In David's house a Saviour rais'd
On His eternal throne;
According to His truth and grace,
To holy prophets known.

3 Salvation's granted by His hand
From all who did us hate;
The mercy is perform'd, for which
Our fathers long did wait.

4 The Covenant with Abr'ham made,
Redemption's grand design,
He hath perform'd the solemn oath,
With grace and truth divine.

5 Thus may we serve Him without fear,
From every terror freed,
In holiness and righteousness,
Our lives before Him lead.

6 Thus like Thy harbinger, O Lord,
Endued with heav'nly grace,
May all Thy priests prepare Thy way
Before Thy glorious face.

7 By the remission of our sin
Make Thy Salvation known,

Rise, Sun of righteousness, on high,
 In tender mercy shewn.

8 Those, who in death and darkness sit,
 With light and comfort bless;
And guide our feet into the way
 Of peace and happiness.

JUBILATE DEO vide Psalm 100.

160

MAGNIFICAT. LUKE 1, 46, &c.

BY BISHOP PATRICK.   L. M.

1 MY soul doth magnify the LORD;
 Transports of joy my spirits raise;
My GOD, my SAVIOUR, Thou shalt be
 The subject of my song of praise.

2 GOD to His humble suppliant's state
 Shew'd mercy, when by woe deprest;
All ages hence His truth shall own,
 And call His favor'd servant blest.

3 The mighty LORD, hath magnified,
 Adored be His holy Name,
His mercy is thro' ev'ry age,
 To them that fear Him still the same.

4 His holy Arm His strength hath shew'd
 Confounded what the proud had thought;
Put down the mighty from their seat
 And rais'd them, who were set at nought.

5 The hungry He hath fill'd with good:
   The full and rich for want complain'd;
His mercy He hath call'd to mind
   And ISRAEL hath His help obtain'd.

6 The promise to our fathers made,
   In which engag'd the Almighty stood,
For EVER sure to Abr'ham's seed,
   GOD hath in sov'reign truth made good.

CANTATE DOMINO vide Psalm. 98.

161

THE SONG OF SIMEON,

NUNC DIMITTIS.   LUKE ii 28, &c.   7. 7.

1 LORD, behold the hour is come,
    Now within the silent tomb
  Let my mortal frame decay,
    Mingled with my kindred clay.

2 Since Thy mercies LORD of old,
    By thy chosen Seers foretold,
  Faithful all and stedfast prove,
    GOD of truth and GOD of love.

3 Sun of righteousness to Thee,
    O let nations bow the knee!
  O let realms of distant kings,
    Own the healing of Thy wings.

4 Hail the light of Jacob's star!
    Spread Thy glories from afar;
  Wide diffuse the gospel ray,
    Ushering in eternal day!

5 On the GENTILES pour Thy light,
    Truth divine in radiance bright!
  On Thy people ISRAEL shine,
    Crown'd with glory all divine.

DEUS MISEREATUR. VIDE PSALM LXVII.

THE FOLLOWING ARRANGEMENT IS MADE ACCORDING TO THE ORDER OF THE LITURGY.

N. B. *The first Psalm specified under each Sunday and Holy Day is the same as was directed by the* Rubric, *in the reign of* King Edward VI. *and was called the* Introit, *because it was sung, while the Priest was going to the Altar.** *The other* Psalms, *or* Hymns *are generally adapted to the* Epistle, *or* Gospel, *or the subject of the day; when there can be no appropriate selection, the arrangement is merely designed to accommodate the choice, and prevent the selection being left to an incompetent person.*

The Psalms referred to at the close of each Sunday, or Holy Day comprise an arrangement of the Psalms throughout the year.

* WHEATLY on the Common Prayer.

ADVENT SUNDAY.

Psalm 1.

Isaiah. lxi i.   C. M.

1 HARK, the glad sound! the Saviour comes,
   The SAVIOUR promis'd long!
Let ev'ry heart prepare a throne,
   And ev'ry voice a song.

2 On Him the Spirit largely pour'd,
   Exerts its sacred fire;
Wisdom and might, and zeal, and love,
   His holy breast inspire.

3 He comes the pris'ners to release,
   In Satan's bondage held;
The gates of brass before Him burst,
   The iron fetters yield.

4 Hear Him, ye deaf; His praise, ye dumb
   Your loosen'd tongues employ;
Ye blind, behold your SAVIOUR come;
   And leap, ye lame, for joy.

5 He comes the broken heart to bind,
   The bleeding soul to cure;
And with the riches of His grace,
   T' enrich the humble poor.

6 Our glad hosannas, Prince of peace,
   Thy welcome shall proclaim;
And heav'n's eternal arches ring
   With thy beloved name.

Psalm xii. cxii. xxii. cxviii. 3 last verses.

The Second Sunday in Advent.

Psalm. CXX.

163   P. M. 8, 7

Luke xxi.—25.—*Rev.* 1—7.

1 LO! He comes with clouds descending,
   Once for favour'd sinners slain :
Thousand thousand saints attending
   Swell the triumph of His train ;
     Hallelujah ! Hallelujah ! Amen.

2 Ev'ry eye shall now behold Him,
   Rob'd in awful majesty ;
Those, who set at nought and sold Him,
   Pierc'd and nail'd Him to the tree,
     Deeply wailing!
   Shall the true Messiah see.

3 Ev'ry island, sea, and mountain,
   Heav'n and earth, shall flee away ;
All who hate Him, must, confounded,
   Hear the trump proclaim the day ;
     Come to judgment !
   Come to judgment ! come away !

4 Now redemption, long expected,
   See in solemn pomp appear !
All His saints by man rejected,
   Now shall meet Him in the air !
     Hallelujah !
   See the day of God appear !

Psalm xcvii—xl—lxxx—ix—xlviii.

The Third Sunday in Advent.

Psalm iv.

164   P. M. 8, 7.

1 RISING from the promis'd nation,
   Lo! the great Messiah's near,
Join in loudest acclamation;
   See the incarnate Son appear!
        Hallelujah!
Saints the joyful tidings hear.

2 He, who laid the world's foundation,
   And the deeps of ocean bound,
Owns to man a near relation,
   And is in a manger found,
        Hallelujah
Praise, eternal praise resound.

3 Lo he comes, th' incarnate Saviour!
   Saints your highest anthems raise;
Love divine, endearing favor,
   Yields ten thousand themes for praise,
        Hallelujah!
Loud resound your heav'nly lays,

4 Strike your harps, the whole creation,
   And a great Redeemer sing;
Join the joyful acclamation,
   And adore the new born King,
        Till to heav'n
Joyful Hallelujah's ring.——

Psalm cxlvi—cxxv—lvii.

THE FOURTH SUNDAY IN ADVENT.

PSALM V.

165

John—i. 1 & 14.   L. M.

1 MY song shall bless the Lord of all,
   My praise shall climb to His abode;
Thee, SAVIOUR, by that name I call,
   The GREAT SUPREME, the MIGHTY GOD.

2 Without beginning or decline,
   Object of faith, and not of sense;
Eternal ages saw him shine,
   He shines eternal ages hence.

3 As much, when in the manger laid,
   Almighty Ruler of the sky,
As when the six day's work he made
   Fill'd all the morning stars with joy.

4 Of all the crowns JEHOVAH bears,
   Salvation is His dearest claim;
That gracious sound well pleas'd He hears,
   And owns EMMANUEL for His name.

Praise GOD from whom all blessings flow &c.

Psalm cxxxii cxxx lxiii cxlviii 2nd met.

CHRISTMAS DAY.

Psalm XCVIII—VIII—CII.

166

Luke ii. 12. 14.   *Sevens*

1 HARK! the herald angels sing,
   Glory to the new born King;
Peace on earth and mercy mild,
God and sinners reconcil'd.

2 Joyful all ye nations rise,
   Join the triumphs of the skies!
With th' angelic host proclaim,
"Christ is born in *Bethlehem !*"

3 Christ, by highest heav'n ador'd,
   Christ, the everlasting Lord;
Late in time behold Him come,
Offspring of the virgin's womb.

4 Veil'd in flesh the Godhead see,
   Hail th' incarnate Deity!
Pleas'd as man with men t'appear:
Jesus our Immanuel here.

5 Hail the heav'n born Prince of peace!
   Hail the Sun of righteousness!
Light and life to all He brings,
Ris'n with healing in His wings!

6 Mild He lays His glory by,
   Born that men no more may die;
Born to raise the sons of earth,
Born to give them second birth.

CHRISTMAS DAY.

167

Luke ii. 8. 14.   P. M. 8, 7.

1 HARK! the harmony of heaven!
   Glory be to GOD on high:
Peace on earth, good will is given,
   Hallelujahs, fill the sky.
Hallelujah!—join the choir,
   Swell the theme, the anthem raise;
Hallelujah! louder, higher,
   Echo round the SAVIOUR's praise.

2 Hark! ten thousand Seraphs praising:
   Hosts unnumber'd laud His name;
Saints in bliss, astonish'd, gazing,
   All IMMANUEL's grace proclaim.
Glory-beams with Godlike favor,
   Hark! glad tidings of great joy!
Lo! for man is born a SAVIOUR,
   Endless praise be man's employ.

3 Joyful news to ev'ry nation,
   MYST'RY great of Bethlehem,
Perfect and complete SALVATION
   To all people in His name!
Lo; He comes, from heav'n descending,
   GOD the SON, th' ETERNAL WORD
Hallelujahs, never ending,
   Be to JESUS CHRIST the LORD.

CHRISTMAS DAY.

Matt. i. 23. L. M.

1 LET angels and archangels sing
    The wonderful IMMANUEL's name;
Adore with us our new-born King,
    And still the joyful news proclaim!
All earth and heav'n be ever join'd
To praise the SAVIOUR of mankind.

2 The everlasting GOD comes down,
    To sojourn with the sons of men,
Without His majesty or crown,
    IMMANUEL (GOD WITH US) is seen
A virgin's womb He did not scorn,
The EVERLASTING SON is born.

3 Angels behold that infant's face,
    With holy awe the Godhead own;
'Tis all your heav'n on Him to gaze,
    And cast your crowns before His throne;
Tho' now He on His footstool lies,
Ye know He built both earth and skies.

4 By Him into existence brought,
    Ye sang the all-creating word:
Ye heard Him call our world from nought;
    Again, in honor of our LORD,
Ye morning stars, your hymns employ;
And shout ye sons of GOD for joy.

St. Stephen's Day,

Psalm LII.

169

Acts vii. 55, L. M.

1 O THOU, that hast redemption wrought !
Patron of souls, Thy blood hath bought !
To Thee our spirits we commit,
Mighty to rescue from the pit.

2 Millions of blissful souls above,
In realms of purity and love,
With songs of endless praise proclaim
The honors of Thy faithful name.

3 When all the pow'rs of nature fail'd,
Thy ever-constant care prevail'd;
Courage and joy Thy mercy spoke,
When ev'ry mortal bond was broke.

4 We on thy mercy, LORD, repose,
The healing balm of all our woes;
And we, when sinking in the grave,
Trust Thine omnipotence to save.

5 O may our spirits, by Thy hand,
Be gather'd to that happy band,
And wait with them that brighter day,
Which all Thy triumph shall display.

St. John's Day.

Psalm XI.

John xxi, 21. 22.　　　　　L. M.

1 LORD, how mysterious are Thy ways!
  How blind are we, how mean our praise
  Thy steps can mortal eyes explore?
  'Tis ours to wonder, and adore.

2 Thy deep decrees from mortal sight
  Are hid in shades of awful night;
  Amid the lines with curious eye
  Not angel minds presume to pry.

3 Great GOD! I would not ask to see
  What in futurity shall be;
  If light and bliss attend my days;
  Then shall my future hours be praise.

4 Is darkness and distress my share?
  Then let me trust Thy guardian care;
  Enough for me, if love divine
  At length thro' ev'ry cloud shall shine.

5 Yet this my soul desires to know,
  Be this my only wish below;
  In life and death, my grand request
  To serve my GOD, and I am blest.

171

INNOCENTS' DAY.

PSALM LXXIX.

171

Matt. ii. 16.   C. M.

1 GREAT GOD, we own Thy sov'reign hand
    Thy faithful care we own;
Wisdom and love are all Thy ways,
    When most to us unknown.

2 By Thee the springs of life are form'd
    And by Thy breath are broke;
And good is evr'y awful word
    Our gracious LORD hath spoke.

3 To Thee we yield our comforts up;
    To Thee our lives resign;
In straits and dangers, rich and safe,
    If we and ours are Thine.

4 Thy saints, in earlier life remov'd,
    In sweeter accents sing,
And bless the swiftness of their flight,
    That bore them to their King.—

5 'The burdens of a lengthen'd day
    With patience may we bear;
And in our dying hours attest
    Thy wisdom, love, and care.

172

SUNDAY AFTER CHRISTMAS DAY.

PSALM CXXI.

172

Luke ii. 13.   C. M.

1 MORTALS awake, with angels join,
　　And chaunt the solemn lay,
Joy, love and gratitude combine
　　To hail th' auspicious day.

2 Hark! the Cherubic armies shout,
　　And glory leads the song:
Good will and peace are heard throughout
　　Th' harmonious heav'nly throng.

3 O for a glance of heav'nly love,
　　Our hearts and tongues to raise;
Sweetly to bear our souls above,
　　And mingle with their lays!

4 With joy the chorus we'll repeat,
　　"Glory to God on high!
"Good will and peace are now complete
　　"Jesus was born to die."

5 Hail, Prince of life, for ever hail!
　　Saviour, Almighty Friend;
Tho' earth, and time, and life should fail,
　　Thy praise shall never end.

Psalm c. xcviii. xxxiv.

NEW YEAR's DAY.

The Circumcision of Christ.

PSALM CXXII. XC. XXXII.

172

Psalm lxv. 11. L. M.

1 ETERNAL Source of ev'ry joy!
O let Thy praise our lips employ,
While in Thy temple we appear,
Thy goodness crowns the circling Year.

2 Seasons renew'd, and years and days,
Demand successive songs of praise;
To Thee be grateful homage paid,
With op'ning light and ev'ning shade.

3 But mercies more than these we own,
Thy mercy in Redemption shewn:
Thy means of grace, whereby we rise
To hopes of glory in the skies.

4 O may we with harmonious tongue
In realms of bliss pursue the song!
There, in those brighter courts adore,
Where days and years revolve no more.

174

PSALM CXXXIX. C. M.

1 WHEN all Thy mercies, O my GOD,
My rising soul surveys,
Transported with the view I'm lost
In wonder, love, and praise.

2 Thy providence my life sustain'd
　And all my wants redrest,
When in the silent womb I lay,
　And hung upon the breast.

3 Unnumber'd comforts to my soul
　Thy tender care bestow'd,
Before my infant heart conceiv'd,
　From whom those blessings flow'd.

4 When in the slipp'ry paths of youth
　With heedless steps I ran,
Thine arm unseen convey'd me safe,
　And led me up to man.

5 When worn by sickness, oft hast Thou,
　With health renew'd my face;
And when in sins and sorrows sunk,
　Reviv'd my soul with grace.

6 Ten thousand thousand precious gifts,
　My daily thanks employ;
O grant me, LORD, a thankful heart,
　To taste those gifts with joy.

7 Thro' ev'ry period of my life
　Thy goodness I'll pursue;
And after death in distant worlds
　The glorious theme renew.

8 When nature fails, and day and night
　Divide Thy works no more;
My ever grateful heart, O LORD,
　Thy mercy shall adore.

9 Thro' all eternity to Thee
　A joyful song I'll raise;
For oh! eternity's too short
　To utter all Thy praise.

175—176

L. M.

1 MY helper God! I bless His name:
The same His pow'r, His grace the same;
The tokens of His friendly care
Open and crown, and close the year.

2 I, midst ten thousand dangers stand,
Supported by His pow'rful hand;
And see, when I survey my ways,
Ten thousand monuments of praise.

3 Thus far His arm hath led me on;
Thus far I make His mercy known;
And, while I tread this desert land,
New mercies shall new songs demand.

4 My grateful soul, on Jordan's shore,
Shall raise one sacred pillar more;
Then bear, in His bright courts above,
Inscriptions of immortal love.

176

1 THIS God is the God we adore,
Our faithful, unchangeable friend;
Whose love is as large as His pow'r,
And neither knows measure, nor end.
Jehovah, the first and the last,
Whose Spirit shall guide us safe home,
We'll praise Him for all that is past,
We'll trust Him for all that's to come.

2 O may we while here we abide,
Attentive be found to Thy will;
The station Thy wisdom assigns
Our portion of duty fulfil.
Since God is our all and in all,
Content or to stay, or remove,
'Tis heav'n to serve Thee below!
To love Thee is heav'n above!

● Psalm xix—xxxiv—cxvi—lxxi.

Epiphany,
or Manifestation of Christ to the Gentiles.

Psalm XCVI. LXXII,
P. M. 8, 7,
Eph. iii. 1. 6.

1 HAIL, Thou Source of ev'ry blessing,
   Sov'reign Father of mankind !
Gentiles now thy grace possessing,
   In Thy courts admission find.
Grateful now we fall before Thee,
   In Thy church obtain a place,
Now by faith behold Thy glory,
   Praise Thy truth, adore Thy grace.

2 Once far off, but now invited,
   We approach Thy sacred throne,
In Thy Covenant united,
   Reconcil'd, redeem'd, made one,
Now reveal'd to eastern sages,
   See the star of mercy shine,
Myst'ry hid in former ages ;
   Myst'ry great of love divine.

3 Hail, Thou universal Saviour !
   Gentiles now their off'rings bring,
In Thy temple seek Thy favor,
   Jesus Christ our Lord and King.
May we, body, soul and spirit,
   Live devoted to Thy praise,
Glorious realms of bliss inherit,
   Grateful anthems ever raise.

178

Mal. iv. 2. L. M.

1 ARISE, O Sun of righteousness,
   The nations of the world to bless;
   With healing in Thy beams arise,
   Display Thy glories thro' the skies.

2 As rain on meadows newly mown,
   So send, O Lord, Thy influence down;
   Thy grace on fainting souls distils
   Like heav'nly dew on thirsty hills.

3 Let heathen lands that lie beneath
   The shades of overspreading death,
   Revive at Thy first dawning light,
   And desarts blossom at the sight.

4 The saints shall flourish in Thy days,
   Drest in the robes of joy and praise,
   Peace, like a river, from Thy throne,
   Shall flow to nations yet unknown.

179

Isaiah lx. 1, 2, 4. P. M. 8, 7,

1 O'ER the gloomy hills of darkness,
   Look my soul, be still, and gaze,
   All the promises do travail
     With a glorious day of grace:
       Hallelujah!
   Let Thy glorious morning dawn.

2 Let the Indian, let the Negro,
   Let the wild Barbarian see
That divine and glorious conquest,
   Once obtain'd on Calvary.
      Let the gospel
Loud resound from pole to pole.

3 Kingdoms wide, that sit in darkness.
   Grant them LORD the glorious light,
And from eastern coast to western,
   May the morning chase the night,
      Hallelujah!
Rise to light eternal day.

4 Fly abroad thou mighty Gospel,
   Spread Thy conquests, never cease;
May Thy lasting wide dominions
   Multiply, and still increase;
      Sway thy Sceptre!
SAVIOUR all the world around.

5 Rise and triumph, favor'd Zion,
   See around the glory shine,
On thee view the Lord arising,
   Cloth'd in brightness all divine;
      Hallelujah!
To Thy light the nations come.

6 Lo! behold the day approaching,
   Day of Jesu's dearness fame!
When the fulness of the Gentiles
   Shall exult to own His name.
      Reign for ever!
KING of Kings, and LORD of Lords!

The First Sunday after Epiphany.

Psalm XIII.

Luke ii. 49. &c.   L. M.

1 MY blest REDEEMER and my LORD!
 I read my duty in Thy word;
But in Thy Life the Law appears
Drawn out in living characters.

2 Such was Thy truth, and such Thy zeal,
Such deff'rence to Thy FATHER's will,
Such love and meekness so divine,
I would transcribe and make them mine.

3 Cold mountains and the midnight air
Witness'd the fervor of Thy pray'r;
The desart Thy temptations knew,
Thy conflict and Thy vict'ry too.

4 Be Thou my pattern, make me bear
More of Thy gracious image here;
Then God the Judge shall own my name
Amongst the follow'rs of the LAMB.

Psalm xxi—cxxviii—cxlviii.

The Second Sunday after Epiphany.

Psalm XIV.

181

Rom. v. 21.   C. M.

1 ARISE, O Lord, reveal Thy face,
   Teach and inspire our tongues
To make Thy sov'reign, reigning grace
   The subject of our songs.
No sweeter subject can invite
   A grateful heart to sing,
Or more display the glorious right
   Of our exalted King.

2 This subject fills the starry plains
   With wonder, joy, and love;
And furnishes the noblest strains
   For all the harps above.
While the redeem'd in praise combine
   To grace upon the throne,
Angels in solemn chorus join,
   And make the theme their own.

3 Lord, when this changing life is past,
   If we may see Thy face,
How shall we praise and love at last,
   And sing Thy truth and grace!
Yet let us aim, while here below,
   Thy mercy to display;
And own, at least, the debt we owe,
   Altho' we ne'er can pay.

Psalm xcv—ciii—cxiii.

THE THIRD SUNDAY AFTER EPIPHANY

PSALM XV.

182

Rom. xv. 11. 12.   L. M.

1 O Thou in whom the Gentiles trust,
  Thou only holy, only just;
  O tune our hearts to praise Thy name,
  JESUS, IMMANUEL the same!

2 If angels, while to Thee they sing,
  Wrap up their faces in their wing;
  How shall we sinful dust draw nigh
  Thy great and awful majesty?

3 Where shall I fit my thankful tongue
  To join with heaven's unnumber'd throng?
  Or how prepare my humble lay,
  Rightly Thy glory to display?

4 Angels alone, and saints above,
  Sinless, and perfected in love,
  Can utter Thy exalted praise,
  And sing the honors of Thy grace.

5 Glory to Thee, auspicious Lamb!
  Thou holy LORD, Thou great I AM!
  Let all our pow'rs unite to bless
  The LORD our strength and righteousness.

6 Live, ever glorious JESUS! live,
  Worthy all blessings to receive!
  Worthy on high enthron'd to sit,
  With ev'ry pow'r beneath Thy feet.

Psalm xxiii. xcii. cxxxii. cxxxiv. 156.

The Fourth Sunday after Epiphany.

Psalm ii.

183

Psalm cxlix.   *(Old 104th.)*

1 O Praise ye the Lord, prepare a new song,
   Assemble, ye saints, the concert to join;
With anthems of triumph the chorus prolong,
   The theme all exalting in praises divine.

2 The Lord on His Church looks down with delight,
   The Lord whom we worship indulgent attends,
Let Zion be joyful, sustain'd by His might,
   While praise from her altars as incense ascends.

3 This honor, ye saints, appointed for you,
   All grateful receive, all faithful obey,
In glory exulting, His will while ye do,
   And make His high praises the theme of
                     [each day.

4 All glory to God! Thy triumphs we sing;
   Eternity shall Thy praises proclaim;
Almighty Redeemer, our Saviour & King,
   For ever and ever adoring Thy name.

Psalm cvii.—cxvii.—157, 159.

THE FIFTH SUNDAY AFTER EPIPHANY.

PSALM XX.

184

Matt. xiii. 24.   S. M.

1 WITH heart and lips unfeign'd,
    We praise Thee for Thy word;
We bless Thee for the joyful sound
    Of our Redemption, LORD.

2 Like as the kindly rain
    Returns not back to heav'n,
But cheers, and fruitful makes the earth,
    The end for which 'twas giv'n.

3 So let Thy holy word
    Accomplish Thy design;
Sow seeds of truth in ev'ry heart,
    And consecrate us Thine.

4 Water the sacred seed,
    And give it great encrease;
Nor let the tares and weeds of sin
    Prevent the fruit of peace.

5 In knowledge bid us grow,
    For Thee our lives employ,
And let the ripen'd harvest yield
    Our souls immortal joy.

Psalm lxvii.—c.—cxxxv.

The Sixth Sunday after Epiphany.

PSALM XXI.

185

Matt, xxiv. 29.   *P. M. 8, 7.*

1 DAY of judgment! day of wonders!
    Hark! the trumpet's awful sound,
Louder than ten thousand thunders,
    Shakes the vast creation round!
      How the summons
    Will the guilty heart confound!

2 See the Judge our nature wearing,
    Cloath'd in majesty divine!
Saints who long for His appearing,
    Then shall shout "*this* GOD *is mine*"
      Gracious SAVIOUR,
    Own me in that day for Thine!

3 Lo 'tis He his Saints desire,
    Come for his redeem'd below!
Come to join us with His choir?
    Come to make our joys o'erflow,
      Palms of vict'ry
    Crowns of glory to bestow!

4 Coming in the clouds of heaven,
    Now His pow'r and glory see;
Saints exult, to you 'tis given
    With Him evermore to be.
      Hallelujah!
    Praise to all eternity.
Psalm lxxxiv. ciii. cxxxvi, 160.

SEPTUAGESIMA SUNDAY.

Psalm XXIII.   C. M.

186

1 WHILE saints above in perfect strains
    Their loud Hosannas raise,
We join the chorus to the LAMB,
    And chaunt His sacred praise.

2 The blissful theme with joy repeat,
    Proclaim His wond'rous love,
Ye saints, who militate below,
    And who adore above.

3 Ye heav'nly choir, who round the throne
    In humble homage bow :
At humble distance, lo, we join,
    Our highest notes with you,

4 Worthy the LAMB enthron'd on high,
    All homage to receive,
More than our pow'rs can e'er return,
    Or thoughts can e'er conceive.

5 Accept our praise 'till we adore,
    With all Thy hosts above ;
And in grand chorus round Thy throne,
    Proclaim that GOD is LOVE.

Psalm xxvii. xcix. civ. cxxxviii.

SEXAGESIMA SUNDAY.

Psalm XXIV.

187

Isaiah lviii. 13.   L. M.

1 WELCOME blest Day, of days the best,
 Design'd of God for holy rest;
When to His house His saints repair,
To offer solemn praise and prayer.

2 This is employment all divine!
My soul the blest assembly join;
Go, bow before Thy Maker's Throne,
And all thy Saviour's glories own.

3 Forget all earthly things and cares,
And soar by faith above the stars;
On wings of strong devotion rise,
And feast on fruits of Paradise.

4 Glory to God, whose love assigns
This sacred rest for wearied minds;
O that our pray'rs and praise may rise,
As grateful incense, to the skies.

5 In holy duties may this day,
In holy pleasures pass away!
And hail that day, while this we spend,
That Sabbath, which will never end.

6 Hail best of days, that God ordain'd,
That man for heaven might be train'd!
Be this my soul thy day of rest;
And thus prepare thee to be blest.

Psalm xxxiv cxiii. cxxxix. cxlv. 158.

QUINQUAGESIMA SUNDAY.

PSALM XXVI.

1 Cor. xiii.   C. M.

1 THO' perfect eloquence adorn
   With sweet persuasive tongue,
Though man could speak in higher strains
   Than ever angel sung:

2 Though liberal gifts the hand imparts;
   Though faith could rocks remove,
It profits nothing, if devoid
   Of charity and love,

3 LOVE suffers long, Love envies not,
   True love is ever kind;
Love glows with social tenderness;
   Love feels for all mankind.

4 Love still shall hold an endless reign,
   In earth, and heav'n above;
When tongues shall cease, and prophets fail,
   And ev'ry gift but love.

5 Now darkly seen, as through a glass,
   Are GOD and truth beheld;
Then shall we see as face to face,
   And GOD shall be unveil'd.

6 Faith, hope and love now dwell on earth,
   And earth by them is blest;
But faith and hope must yield to love,
   Of all the graces best.

7 Hope shall to full fruition rise,
   Faith lost in sight above:
But love shall triumph to the end;
   The heav'n of heav'ns is LOVE.

Psalm xlcv. cxxvi. cxlviii. 152.

ASH WEDNESDAY.

PSALM VI. C. M.

The lamentation of a sinner.*

189

1 O LORD, turn not Thy face away
   From him that lies prostrate,
Lamenting sore his many sins,
   Before Thy mercy's gate,

2 LORD, I come to Thy throne of grace,
   Where mercy doth abound,
Desiring mercy for my sins,
   To heal my soul's deep wound.

3 The circumstances of my sins,
   Their number and their kind,
Thou know'st them all, and more, much more
   Than I can call to mind.

4 O LORD, I need not to repeat,
   What I do beg and crave;
For Thou dost know, before I ask,
   The thing that I would have.

5 Mercy, good LORD, mercy I ask,
   This is the total sum;
For mercy, LORD, is all my suit,
   LORD, let Thy mercy come.

Psalm xxxix. cxlii. cxlvi 163.

* From the Old Version.

THE FIRST SUNDAY IN LENT.

Psalm XXXII. LI.

190   L. M.

1 GREAT Judge of all, Eternal King!
   Thou mercy's unexhausted spring!
To Thee my contrite heart I rend,
My GOD! my SAVIOUR! and my FRIEND!

2 Surrounded with amazing fears,
I sigh and weep, accept my tears;
Reject not my unworthy prayer;
My guilty soul in mercy spare.

3 Thou, who for man didst feel such pain;
Whose precious blood the cross did stain,
Forget not what my ransom cost,
Nor let my dear-bought soul be lost.

4 Thou, who wert mov'd with Mary's grief
Thou, who absolv'd a dying thief,
Grant me at thy right hand a place,
A sinner sav'd alone by grace.

5 My GOD, what interest can I make,
Where else can I for refuge take?
Where but in Thee, Friend of mankind,
Can guilty man such mercy find?*

Psalm xlii. ciii.

‡ Altered from Lord Roscommon's Dies Iræ.

The Second Sunday in Lent.

Psalm CXXX.

191

Heb. iv. 14, &c.   C. M,

1 WITH joy we meditate the grace
    Of our High Priest above:
His heart is made of tenderness,
    Of faithfulness and love.

2 Touch'd with a sympathy within,
    He knows our feeble frame;
He knows what sore temptations mean,
    For He hath felt the same.

3 He, in the days of feeble flesh,
    Pour'd out strong cries and tears: *Heb.* v. 7.
And in His measure feels afresh,
    What ev'ry member bears.

4 He'll never quench the smoking flax,
    But raise it to a flame:
The bruised reed He never breaks,
    Nor scorns the meanest name.

5 Then, let our humble faith address
    His mercy and His pow'r:
We shall obtain deliv'ring grace,
    In the distressing hour.

Psalm i. xli. lxxxvi. cviii. cxi.

192

THE THIRD SUNDAY IN LENT.

PSALM XLIII.

192   C, M.

Psalm v. 7.

1 O PRAISE the LORD, unite to praise
    The SAVIOUR of mankind.
Our thankful hearts in solemn lays
    Be with our voices join'd.

2 But how shall dust His worth declare,
    When angels try in vain;
Their faces veil when they appear
    Before the Son of man.

3 O LORD we cannot silent be,
    By love we are constrain'd
To offer our best thanks to Thee—
    Our SAVIOUR, and our Friend!

4 Tho' feeble are our best essays,
    Thy love will not despise,
Our grateful songs of humble praise,
    Our well meant sacrifice.

5 Let ev'ry tongue Thy goodness show,
    And spread abroad Thy fame:
Let ev'ry heart with praise o'erflow,
    And bless Thy sacred name.

6 Worship and honor, thanks and love,
    To JESUS CHRIST be giv'n!
By men below,—by hosts above,—
    By all in earth and heav'n!

Psalm xlii—lxxxvi—cxii-

The Fourth Sunday in Lent.

Psalm XLVII.

193.

Luke xviii. 13.   C. M.

1 PROSTRATE, blest Saviour, at Thy feet
   A guilty sinner lies;
And upwards to the mercy seat
   Presumes to lift his eyes.

2 O let not justice frown me hence;
   Stay, stay the vengeful storm;
Forbid it that Omnipotence
   Should crush a feeble worm.

3 If tears of sorrow would suffice,
   To pay the debt I owe,
Tears should from both my weeping eyes
   In ceaseless torrents flow.

4 But no such sacrifice I plead
   To expiate my guilt;
No tears but those that Thou hast shed,
   No blood but Thou hast spilt.

5 Think of Thy sorrows gracious Lord,
   And all my sins forgive:
Justice will well approve the word
   That bids the sinner live.

    Psalm lxiii—xcv—cxxvi—cxlvii.

THE FIFTH SUNDAY IN LENT.

PSALM. LIV.

194 L. M.

1 Cor. xv. 45.

1 LORD, in the dust, before Thy throne,
  Our guilt and our disgrace we own;
  Great GOD, we own th' unhappy name,
  Whence sprung our nature, and our shame.

2 But whilst our spirits fill'd with awe,
  Behold the terrors of Thy Law,
  We sing the honors of Thy grace,
  That sent to save our ruin'd race.

3 We sing Thine everlasting SON,
  Who join'd our nature to His own:
  ADAM, the second, from the dust
  Raises the ruins of the first.

4 Where sin did reign, and death abound,
  There have the sons of ADAM found
  Abounding life, there glorious grace
  Reigns thro' the LORD our RIGHTEOUSNESS.

5 All blessings, might and majesty,
  Then to our GOD for ever be;
  To JESUS CHRIST our SAVIOUR raise,
  Eternal songs of endless praise.

Psalm li. lxv. ciii. cxiii.

PALM SUNDAY.

PSALM LX. XX.

195   P. M. 8, 7.

Heb. ix. 11, 12.

1 HAIL! Thou once despised Jesus!
   Hail! Thou Galilean King!
Who didst suffer to release us,
   Who didst free salvation bring!
Hail! Thou glorious GOD and SAVIOUR,
   Who hast born our sin and shame,
By whose merits we find favor,
   Life is given thro' Thy name!

2 Paschal LAMB, by GOD appointed,
   All our sins were on Thee laid!
By Almighty love anointed,
   Thou hast full atonement made;
Every sin may be forgiven,
   Thro' the virtue of Thy blood,
Open'd is the gate of heaven,
   Peace is made 'twixt man and GOD.

3 Jesus hail! enthron'd in glory,
   There for ever to abide,
All the heav'nly hosts adore Thee,
   Seated at Thy Father's side;
There for sinners thou art pleading,
   "Spare them yet another year"—
There for saints art interceding,
   'Till in glory they appear.

4 Worship, honor, pow'r and blessing,
   CHRIST is worthy to receive—
Loudest praises without ceasing,
   Meet it is for us to give!
Help ye bright angelic spirits,
   Bring your sweetest noblest lays,
Help to sing our SAVIOUR's merits,
   Help to chaunt IMMANUEL's praise.

Psalm xvi. 2nd. part.

MONDAY BEFORE EASTER.

196   L. M.

Phil. ii. 8, *Col* ii. 15,

1 THE mighty frame of glorious grace,
   That brightest monument of praise!
That e'er th' Eternal GOD design'd,
Employs and fills my lab'ring mind.

2 Begin, my soul, the heav'nly song,
   A subject for an angel's tongue :
When angels sound these awful things
They tune and summon all their strings.

3 Proclaim inimitable love,
   JESUS, the Lord of worlds above,
Puts off the beams of bright array,
And veils the GOD in mortal clay.

4 He that distributes crowns and thrones,
   Hangs on a tree, and bleeds, and groans,
The Prince of life resigns His breath,
The King of glory bows to death.

5 Behold the wonders of His power,
 Christ triumphs in His dying hour!
 Our life He purchas'd when He fell
 And overcame the pow'rs of hell.

6 Thus were the hosts of death subdued,
 And sin aton'd by Jesu's blood:
 Then He arose and reigns above,
 And conquers sinners by His love.

TUESDAY BEFORE EASTER.

1 INFINITE grace almighty love!
 Stand in amaze, ye rolling skies!
 Jesus, the Lord, extends His arms
 Upon a cross of love, and dies!

2 Did ever pity stoop so low,
 Dress'd in divinity and blood?
 Well may the Church triumphant bow,
 And sing to their incarnate God.

3 There glory shines in every face;
 There friendship shines in ev'ry eye;
 There shall our tongues relate the grace
 That led us homeward to the sky.

4 O'er all the names of Christ our King
 Shall our melodious voices rove:
 Our harps shall sound, from ev'ry string.
 The wonders of His dying love.

5 O Lord, for bounty so divine
 We ne'er can equal honors raise!
 Saviour, may all our hearts be Thine,
 And all our tongues proclaim Thy praise!

198

WEDNESDAY BEFORE EASTER.

198   L. M.

Isaiah liii. 31.—*Gal.* vi. 14.

1 ARISE, my soul; with wonder see
    What love divine for thee hath done!
Behold thy sorrows, sin, and grief,
    Are laid on GOD's Eternal SON.

2 See! from His head, His hands, His feet,
    Sorrow and love flow mingling down;
Did e'er such love, such sorrow meet,
    Or thorns compose so bright a crown!

3 My soul, survey the wond'rous cross,
    On which the Prince of glory died,
And count thy richest gain but loss,
    And pour contempt on all thy pride.

4 Forbid it LORD, that I should boast,
    Save in the cross of CHRIST my GOD;
All the vain things that please me most,
    I'd sacrifice them to His blood.

5 Were the whole realm of nature mine,
    That were a present far too small;
Love so amazing, so divine,
    Demands my soul, my life my all.

199

Thursday before Easter.

199

Zech. xiii. 7.   L. M.

1 "Awake, O sword," the Father cries;
   The sword awakes, and Jesus dies;
He bows His head beneath the stroke,
To free our souls from Satan's yoke.

2 What mingled dignity and grace
Appear'd in our Redeemer's face,
When He forsook the courts above,
And swiftly flew on wings of love!

3 Our nature with His own He joins,
And thus fulfils His grand designs;
The Son of man, the Son of God,
Redeems the Church with His own blood.

4 How great the price Messiah paid,
When He His soul an off'ring made!
Behold redemption all complete!
Behold the Saviour's love how great!

5 See grace and justice both combine!
United now, how bright they shine!
God's glory in the cross appears,
And Mercy's voice dispels our fears.

GOOD FRIDAY.

PSALM XXII.

200

Isaiah liii.

1 WHO hath our report believed?
　　Shiloh come, is not received.
　　　Not received by His own;
　Promis'd branch from root of Jesse,
　David's offspring sent to bless ye,
　　　Comes too meekly to be known.

2 Like a tender plant that's growing
　Where no water's friendly flowing,
　　　No kind rains refresh the ground:
　Drooping, dying we shall view Him,
　See no charm to draw us to Him,
　　　There no beauty will be found.

3 Lo! Messiah unrespected,
　Man of griefs, despised, rejected;
　　　Wounds His form disfiguring,
　Marr'd His visage more than any,
　For He bears the sins of many.
　　　All our sorrows carrying.

4 No deceit His mouth hath spoken,
　Blameless, He no law had broken;
　　　Yet was number'd with the worst;
　For, because the LORD would grieve Him,
　We who saw it, did believe Him
　　　For His own offences curst.

5 But while him our thoughts accused,
 He for us alone was bruised,
  Stricken, smitten for our guilt :
 With His stripes our wounds are cured,
 By His pains our peace assured,
  Purchas'd with the blood He spilt.

6 Love amazing, so to mind us,
 Shepherd come from heaven to find us,
  Wand'ring sheep all gone astray !
 Lost, undone by our transgressions!
 Worse than stript of all possessions,
  Debtors without hope to pay.

7 Fear our portion, slaves in spirit,—
 He redeem'd us by His merit,
  To a glorious liberty :
 Dearly first His goodness brought us,
 Truth and love then sweetly taught us:
  Truth and love have made us free.

8 Blessed be the pow'r who gave us,
 Freely gave His Son to save us ;
  Bless'd the Son, who freely came:
 Honor, blessing, adoration,
 Ever from the whole creation,
  Be to God, and to the Lamb,

GOOD FRIDAY.

John. xix. 30.   8, 7.

1 HARK! the voice of love and mercy
　　Sounds aloud from *Calvary*;
　See! it rends the rocks asunder,
　　Shakes the earth and veils the sky!
　　　"IT IS FINISH'D!"
　Hear the dying SAVIOUR cry!

2 IT IS FINISH'D! O what pleasure
　　Do these sacred words afford!
　Heav'nly blessings without measure
　　Flow to us from CHRIST the LORD.
　　　IT IS FINISH'D!
　Saints the dying words record.

3 FINISH'D all the types and shadows
　　Of the ceremonial law!
　Finish'd all that GOD had promis'd,
　　Death and hell no more shall awe.
　　　IT IS FINISH'D!
　Saints, from hence your comfort draw.

4 Tune your harps anew, ye seraphs,
　　Join to sing the glorious theme!
　All on earth, and all in heaven,
　　Join to praise IMMANUEL's name.
　　　Hallelujah!
　Glory to the bleeding LAMB.

GOOD FRIDAY.

Matt. xxvii. 45, 46. C. M.

1 ALAS! and did my Saviour bleed?
   And did my Sov'reign die?
 Would he devote that sacred head
   For such a worm as I?

2 Was it for crimes that I had done
   He groan'd upon the tree?
 Amazing pity! grace unknown!
   And love beyond degree.

3 Well might the sun in darkness hide,
   And shut his glories in;
 When the Almighty Saviour died
   For man the creature's sin.

4 Thus might I hide my blushing face,
   While Jesu's cross appears,
 Dissolve my heart in thankfulness,
   And melt my eyes to tears.

5 But drops of grief can ne'er repay
   The debt of love I owe;
 Here Lord, I give my self to Thee,
   'Tis all that I can do.

203.

John. iii. 14. 15.   S. M.

1 BEHOLD th' amazing sight,
    The Saviour lifted high!
  Behold the Son of God's delight
    Expire in agony!

2 For whom, for whom, my heart,
    Were all those sorrows borne?
  Why did He feel that piercing smart,
    And meet that various scorn?

3 For love of us He bled,
    And all in torture died:
  'Twas love that bow'd His fainting head,
    And ope'd His streaming side.

4 Lord help me to adore
    In sympathy of love;
  To feel the strong attractive pow'r
    To lift my soul above.

5 Drawn by such cords as these,
    Let all the earth combine,
  With holy ardour to confess
    The Mystery divine.

6 In Thee our hearts unite,
    Nor share Thy griefs alone,
  But from Thy cross pursue their flight
    To Thy triumphant Throne.

EASTER-EVEN.

Psalm LXXXVIII.   C. M.

1 BEHOLD the Saviour of mankind,
   Omnipotent to save!
Behold what love His heart inclin'd;
   Submissive to the grave.

2 When He expir'd all nature shook,
   Earth's strongest pillars bent;
The temple's veil asunder broke,
   The opening graves were rent.

3 "Tis finish'd! now the ransom's paid—
   Receive my soul, He cried:
'Twas then He bow'd His sacred head,
   He bow'd His head and died.

4 Soon will He break death's envious chain,
   And in full glory shine;
O Lamb of God! was ever pain,
   Was ever love like Thine!

5 Learn, O my soul, from this dire scene
   How vast that guilt must be,
Which nail'd th' incarnate Son of God
   To the accursed tree.

6 Taught by this scene, thy sin bewail
   With penitential sighs;
And trust His grace, thro' death's dark vale
   To guide thee to the skies.

EASTER SUNDAY.

—▶•▶•◆•◀•◀—

PSALM XVI. II. CXVIII.   7, 7.

205

1 JESUS CHRIST is ris'n to-day—Hallelujah!
　Our triumphant holy-day;
Who so lately on the cross
Suffer'd to redeem our loss.

2 Hymns of praises let us sing,
Unto CHRIST, our heav'nly King,
Who endur'd the cross and grave,
Sinners to redeem and save.

3 By the pains, which He endur'd
Our salvation is procur'd;
Now above the sky He's King,
Where the angels ever sing.—Hallelujah!

206

Heb. xix. 20, 21.   C. M.

1 GREAT GOD of peace and GOD of love!
　We own Thy pow'r to save.
All hail! great Shepherd of the sheep!
Victorious o'er the grave.

2 Him from the dead, Thou brought'st again,
When by His sacred blood,

Confirm'd and seal'd for evermore.
Th' eternal Cov'nant stood.

3 Strengthen, O LORD, our feeble souls,
Conform us to Thy will;
Settle our hearts to stray no more,
But keep Thy precepts still.

4 Glory to Thee, Great Son OF GOD,
Glory to Thee be giv'n,
For ever, and for evermore,
Thro' all the days of heav'n.

207

Matt. xxviii.   7, 7.

1 CHRIST THE LORD is ris'n to-day
Sons of men and angels say;
Raise your joys and triumphs high,
Sing ye heav'ns, and earth reply.

2 Love's redeeming work is done,
Fought the fight, the battle won;
Lo! our Sun's eclipse is o'er,
Lo! He sets in blood no more.

3 Vain the stone, the watch, the seal,
CHRIST hath burst the gates of hell;
Death in vain forbids His rise,
CHRIST hath open'd Paradise.

3 Lives again our glorious King,
Where, O death is now thy sting?
Once He died our souls to save,
Where's thy victory, O grave?

5 May we rise where CHRIST hath led,
Following our exalted Head;
In His image may we rise.
Our's the cross, the grave, the skies.

6 King of glory! soul of bliss,
Everlasting life is this—
Thee to know—Thy pow'r to prove,
Thee to serve, adore, and love.

208

Psalm cxviii, 24. • Old 148th.

1 ALL hail! triumphant LORD!
To Thee all praise belongs;
The wonders of this day
Demand our noblest songs.
Auspicious morn! thy blissful rays,
Bright Seraphs hail in songs of praise.

2 At thy approaching dawn,
Reluctant Death resign'd
The glorious Prince of life,
Her dark domains confin'd.
Th' angelic host around Him bends,
And 'midst their shouts, the GOD ascends.

3 All hail! triumphant LORD!
Heav'n with Hosannas rings;
While earth, in humbler strains,
Thy praise responsive sings:
Worthy art Thou, who once wast slain,
Thro' endless years to live and reign.

209

Rev. i. 18. S. M.

1 JESUS, who once was dead,
The LAMB for sinners slain;
He lives, and lives for evermore,
O'er death and hell to reign.

2 Rejoice, ye saints, and sing,
　His love and pow'r proclaim;
Ten thousand, thousand praises bring.
　In honor of His name.

210

Matt. xxviii. 6.　　Old 112th.

1 THE Lord, is risen! He who came
　　To suffer death and conquer too:
The Lord is risen! loud proclaim
　　The praise to our REDEEMER due:
He lives, He lives, who once was dead—
Let glory crown the Conq'ror's head,

2 The Lord is ris'n to His abode;
　　Aided by grace, be our employ
To die to sin, to live to God;
　　To serve with fear and holy joy.
He lives, He lives, who once was dead—
Let glory crown the Conq'ror's head.

3 The Lord is ris'n! let hosts above,
　　Triumphant now, proclaim His praise;
Let saints on earth adore His love,
　　And consecrate to him their days.
He lives, He lives, who once was dead—
Let glory crown the Conq'ror's head.

4 When life is past, when time is o'er,
　　O may we all to glory rise;
There dwell with Him for evermore,
　　With countless myriads in the skies,
And sing his praise, who once was dead,
And ever crown our Conq'ror's head.

Monday in Easter Week.

Psalm LXII.

211

Psalm xvi. 9. 12.

WHEN I the holy grave survey,
  Where once my Saviour deign'd to lie,
I see fulfill'd what prophets say,
  And all the powr's of death defy.

2 This empty tomb shall now proclaim
  How weak the bands of conquer'd death;
Sweet pledge, that all who trust His name
  Shall rise, and draw immortal breath!

3 Our surety freed, declares us free,
  For whose offences He was seiz'd;
Our pardon in his hands we see,
  And shout to view Jehovah pleas'd.

4 Jesus, once number'd with the dead,
  Unseals His eyes, to sleep no more,
And ever lives our cause to plead,
  For whom the pains of death He bore.

5 Thy risen Lord, my soul adore,
  See the rich diadem He wears!
Thou too shalt bear an harp of gold,
  To crown thy joy when He appears.

6 Tho' in the dust I lay my head,
  Yet, gracious God, Thou wilt not leave
My flesh for ever with the dead,
  Nor lose Thy children in the grave.

f

Tuesday in Easter Week.

Psalm CXIII.

212 L. M.

1 LET joyful nations hail the day,
    That crowns their King with loud acclaim:
  Let saints their grateful homage pay
    To their Almighty Saviour's name.
  Resound, resound in joyful strains,
  Jesus the King of glory reigns!

2 Sing how He vanquish'd all your foes;
    He came to save, He reigns to bless;
  From Him our ev'ry comfort flows,
    Life, liberty, and joy, and peace.
  Resound, resound in joyful strains,
  Jesus the King of glory reigns!

3 Yes, Thou art worthy, gracious Lord,
    Of universal, endless praise;
  With ev'ry pow'r to be ador'd,
    That men or angels e'er can raise.
  Resound, resound in joyful strains,
  Jesus the King of glory reigns!

4 He comes, He comes, with triumph crown'd
    In dazzling robes of light array'd:
  Faith views the splendor dawning round,
    Earth's fairest lustre sinks in shade.
  Resound, resound in joyful strains,
  Jesus the King of glory reigns.

The First Sunday after Easter.

Psalm CXII.

213

1 Cor. xv. 20, 21. 55. L. M.

1 HE dies! the Friend of sinners dies!
  Lo! Salem's daughters weep around!
A solemn darkness veils the skies,
  A sudden trembling shakes the ground!
Come, saints, and drop a tear or two,
  For Him who groan'd beneath your load!
He shed a thousand drops for you,
  A thousand drops of richer blood.

2 Here's love and grief beyond degree,
  The Lord of glory dies for men!
But lo! what sudden joys we see!
  Jesus the dead revives again!
The rising God forsakes the tomb!
  The tomb in vain forbids His rise!
Cherubic legions guard Him home,
  And shout Him welcome to the skies!

3 Break off your tears, ye saints! and tell
  How high our great Deliv'rer reigns!
Sing how he spoil'd the hosts of hell,
  And led the monster death in chains.
Say, " live for ever wond'rous King!
  " Born to redeem, and strong to save!"
Then ask the monster—"Where's thy sting?
  "And where's thy vict'ry, boasting grave?"

Psalm xxiv. xlviii. lxxii. 179.

THE SECOND SUNDAY AFTER EASTER.

PSALM LXX. XXIII.

214

1 Pet. ii. 24. L. M.

1 WHAT shall we render unto Thee,
  Thou glorious LORD of life and pow'r!
 Teach us to bow the humble knee:
  Teach us with thankfulness t'adore;
 To praise Thee as Thy saints above,
 To praise Thee for Thy woud'rous love.

2 When like lost sheep we wander'd wide,
  And left the watchful Shepherd's eye;
 When borne along th' impetuous tide
  Of this world's sin and vanity:
 Our SAVIOUR then from heav'n came down,
 To save us by His grace alone.

3 He bore our sins upon the tree,
  To seek and save the lost he came;
 There was He bound to set us free
  From death and everlasting shame;
 The captive flock from hell was freed,
 And ransom'd when their Shepherd bled.

4 Then shall our grateful songs abound
  And ev'ry tear be wip'd away;
 No sin, no sorrow shall be found,
  No night o'ercloud the endless day;
 O praise Him! all beneath, above!
 O praise Him! praise the GOD of love?

Psalm lvii. lxvi. cx.

The third Sunday after Easter.

Psalm LXXV.

1 GLORY to God on high!
Let earth and skies reply;
   Praise ye His name:
His love and grace adore,
Who all our sorrows bore,
Sing aloud evermore,
   Worthy the Lamb.

2 Jesus, our Lord and God,
Bore sin's tremendous load,
   Praise ye His name;
Tell what His arm hath done,
What spoils from death He won;
Sing His great name alone;
   Worthy the Lamb.

3 While they around the throne
Cheerfully join in one
   Praising His name;
Ye who believe His blood
Doth seal your peace with God,
Proclaim His grace abroad,
   Worthy the Lamb.

4 Then let the hosts above,
In realms of endless love,
   Praise His blest name;
To him ascribed be
Honor and majesty,
Thro' all eternity
   Worthy the Lamb.
     Psalm ii. lxiii. xcviii.

The fourth Sunday after Easter.

Psalm LXXVIII.

216

   2 Cor. iv. 6.   L. M.

1 SING to the Lord a noble song!
 Awake, my soul; awake my tongue;
Hosanna to th' eternal name,
And all His boundless love proclaim.

2 See where it shines in Jesu's face,
The brightest image of His grace;
God, in the person of his Son,
Hath all His mightiest works out-done.

3 The spacious earth, and spreading flood,
Proclaim the wise and pow'rful God:
And Thy rich glories from afar,
Sparkle in every rolling star.

4 But in Thy looks a glory stands,
The noblest labor of Thy hands;
Redemption beaming in His eyes,
Out-shines the wonders of the skies.

5 Grace! O divine, ennobling theme;
My thoughts rejoice in Jesu's name,
Ye angels, dwell upon the sound;
Ye heav'ns, reflect it to the ground.

6 O, may I live to reach the place
Where He unveils His sacred face!
Where all His glories you behold,
And sing His name to harps of gold.
    Psalm lxv. lxxi.

The Fifth Sunday after Easter.

Psalm LXXXVII.

217   P. M. 8, 7.

1 MIGHTY God, while Angels praise Thee,
    Saints on earth may chaunt Thy name;
Lord of men as well as angels!   [Amen.
Thou art ev'ry creature's theme. Hallelujah,

2 Lord of ev'ry land and nation,
    Ancient of eternal days!
Sounded through the wide creation
    Be Thy just and lawful praise.   Hal.

3 Author of the great Redemption,
    Glorious mystery of love!
God propitious, sin forgiv'n,
    God incarnate from above!   Hal.

4 From the highest throne of glory,
    To the cross of deepest woe;
All to ransom guilty captives,
    Flow my praise, for ever flow.   Hal.

5 Rise to bliss, immortal Saviour,
    Leave Thy footstool, take Thy throne!
Thence return and reign for ever,
    Be the kingdom all Thy own.   Hal.

6 Grant we may behold Thy glory,
    Grant us, Lord, in Heav'n a place;
There to cast our crowns before Thee,
    Lost in wonder, love, and praise.
    Hallelujah, Amen.

Psalm xx. cxlix. cl.

ASCENSION DAY.

PSALM XLVII. XXI.

Psalm xxiv.   L. M.

1 OUR LORD is risen from the dead,
    MESSIAH is gone up on high;
The pow'rs of hell are captive led,
    Dragg'd to the portals of the sky.

2 There His triumphal chariot waits,
    And angels chaunt the solemn lay;
Lift up your heads, ye heav'nly gates,
    Ye everlasting doors give way!

3 Loose all your bars of massy light,
    And wide unfold th' etherial scene;
He claims these mansions as His right,
    Receive the king of glory in!

4 Who is the King of glory, who?
    The LORD, who all our foes o'ercame;
The world, sin, death, and hell o'erthrew.
    And JESUS is the Conqu'ror's name.

5 Lo! His triumphal chariot waits,
    And Angels chaunt the solemn lay;
Lift up your heads, ye heav'nly gates,
    Ye everlasting doors give way!

6 Who is the King of glory, who?
    The LORD of glorious pow'r possest;
The King of saints and angels too,
    GOD over all, for ever blest!

John xvii. 24. C. M.

1 AWAKE, my soul, and grateful sing
    Th' ascended SAVIOUR's love:
Sing how he lives to carry on
    His people's cause above.

2 With cries and tears He offer'd up
    His humble suit below;
But with authority He asks,
    Enthron'd in glory now.

3 For all that come to GOD by Him,
    Salvation He demands;
Points to their names upon His breast,
    And spreads His wounded hands.

4 Eternal life, at His request,
    To ev'ry saint is giv'n:
Safety on earth, and after death,
    The plenitude of heav'n.

5 Founded on right, Thy prayer avails,
    The FATHER smiles on Thee;
And now Thou in Thy kingdom art,
    O LORD, remember me.

6 Let the sweet incense of Thy prayer
    In my behalf ascend;
And as its virtue, so my praise
    Shall never, never, end.

SUNDAY AFTER ASCENSION DAY.

PSALM XCIII.

C. M.

1 O The delights, the heav'nly joys,
    The glories of the place,
Where Jesus sheds the brightest beams
    Of His o'erflowing grace!

2 Sweet majesty and awful love
    Sit smiling on His brow;
While all the glorious ranks above
    At humble distance bow.

3 Hosanna to our conq'ring King!
    All hail, incarnate love!
Ten thousand thousand glories wait,
    To crown Thy head above!

4 Arch-angels sound His lofty praise
    Through ev'ry heav'nly street;
And lay their highest honors down
    Submissive at His feet.

5 That ever blest majestic head,
    Which cruel thorns did wound;
See, what immortal glories shine,
    And circle it around.

6 This is th' eternal Son of God,
    Whom we unseen adore:
But when our eyes behold His face,
    Our hearts shall love Him more.

7 Now to the LAMB, that once was slain,
    Be endless honors paid;
  Salvation, glory, joy, remain,
    For ever on Thy head.

· Psalm lxviii. cx.

221

Heb. ix. 24. C. M.

1 LIFT up your eyes to th' heav'nly seats,
    Where your REDEEMER stays;
  Kind intercessor, there He sits,
    And loves, and pleads, and prays.

2 'Twas well my soul, He died for thee,
    And shed His vital blood;
  Appeas'd stern justice on the tree,
    And then arose to GOD.

3 Petitions now and praise may rise,
    And saints their off'rings bring;
  The Priest with His own sacrifice
    Presents them to the King.

4 Ten thousand praises to the King,
    Hosanna in the high'st!
  Ten thousand thanks our spirits bring
    To GOD and to His CHRIST.

WHIT-SUNDAY.

Psalm XXXIII. LXVIII.

Extracted from the Ordination Office. L. M.

1 COME Holy Ghost, our souls inspire,
　And lighten with celestial fire.
Thou the anointing spirit art,
　Who dost Thy sev'n-fold gifts impart.

2 Thy blessed unction from above,
　Is comfort, life, and fire, of love,
Enable with perpetual light
　The dulness of our blinded sight.

3 Anoint and chear our soiled face,
　With the abundance of Thy grace,
Keep far our foes, give peace at home!
　Where Thou art guide, no ill can come.

4 Teach us to know the Father, Son,
　And Thee, of both, to be but one;
That through the ages all along,
　This, this may be our endless song.

5 Praise God, from whom all blessings flow,
　Praise Him all creatures here below:
Praise Him above, ye heav'nly host,
　Praise Father, Son, and Holy Ghost

Altered from the Old Version, entitled a Prayer to the Holy Ghost, to be sung before the Sermon

C. M

1 COME Holy Spirit, God of might,
    Great comforter of all;
Teach us to know Thy word aright,
    That we may never fall.

2 O Lord, that gav'st Thy holy word,
    Send preachers plenteously;
And in the same may we accord,
    And therein live and die.

3 O Holy Spirit, guide aright
    The preachers of Thy word;
Satan dethrone, and sin subdue,
    By Thy almighty sword.

4 Depart not from Thy pastors, Lord
    Supply their ev'ry need;
They break to us the bread of life,
    Grant us thereon to feed.

5 Convert all those, who know not God,
    And bring them to Thy light;
May Thy whole Church in truth agree,
    And praise Thee day and night.

6 O Lord of Hosts increase our faith,
    And let our love abound;
To distant nations send Thy truth
    Thro' the whole world around.

VENI CREATOR.

From the new Version. C. M.

1 COME, Holy Ghost, Creator, come,
    Inspire the souls of Thine
  Till ev'ry heart which thou hast made
    Is fill'd with grace divine.
  Thou art the Comforter, the gift
    Of God, and fire of love :
  The everlasting spring of joy,
    And unction from above.

2 Thy gifts are manifold. Thou writ'st
    God's Laws in each true heart :
  The promise of the Father, Thou
    Dost heav'nly speech impart.
  Enlighten our dark souls, till they
    Thy sacred love embrace:
  Assist our minds by nature frail,
    With Thy celestial grace.

3 With Thee, O Father, therefore may
    The Son, from death restor'd,
  And sacred Comforter, one God,
    Devoutly be ador'd.
  As in all ages heretofore
    Has constantly been done;
  As now it is, and shall be so,
    When Time his course has run.

VENI CREATOR. L. M.

1 CREATOR, SPIRIT, by whose aid
The world's foundations first were laid
Come visit ev'ry waiting mind,
Come, pour Thy joys on human-kind;
From sin and sorrow set us free
And make us temples meet for Thee.

2 Hail, Source of uncreated light!
Illumine our dull, darken'd sight.
Thrice holy Fount, immortal Fire,
Our hearts with heav'nly love inspire;
Come and Thy sacred unction bring
To sanctify us, while we sing.

3 O GOD of mercy, truth and love,
Now shed Thy influence from above;
Unfailing comfort, heav'nly Guide,
Now o'er Thy favor'd Church preside;
And still from age to age convey
The glory of this sacred day.

4 Immortal honor, endless fame,
Attend th' almighty FATHER'S name;
The SAVIOUR SON, be glorified,
Who for lost man's redemption died;
And equal adoration be
Eternal COMFORTER, to Thee.

MONDAY IN WHITSUN WEEK.

226

P. M.

1 HOLY GHOST! inspire our praises,
 Shed abroad a SAVIOUR's love;
While we chaunt the name of JESUS,
Deign on ev'ry heart to move.
Source of sweetest consolation!
Breathe Thy peace on all below;
Bless, O bless this congregation,
Bid our hearts with influence glow.

2 Come with heav'nly inspiration,
JESUS in our souls reveal;
Manifest this great salvation,
As Thy own our spirits seal.
Light divine, on darkness shining,
Deign the light of truth to give;
Every grace and joy combining,
May we to Thy glory live.

3 Hail, ye spirits bright and glorious,
High exalted round the throne!
Now with you we join in chorus,
And your LORD we call our own.
GOD to us His SON hath given:
Saints your noblest anthems raise!
All in earth and all in heaven,
Shout the great JEHOVAH's praise!

TUESDAY IN WHITSUN WEEK.

227

S. M.

1 COME, HOLY SPIRIT; come;
   Let Thy bright beams arise:
Dispel the sorrow from our mind,
   The darkness from our eyes.

2   Cheer our desponding hearts,
   With visitations sweet;
Give us to lie with humble hope,
   At our REDEEMER's feet.

3   Revive our drooping faith,
   Our doubts and fears remove;
And kindle in our hearts the flame
   Of never-dying love.

4   Convince us of our sin,
   Then lead to JESU's blood;
And to our wond'ring view reveal
   Th' amazing love of GOD.

5   Shew us the sinner's Friend,
   That rules the courts of bliss;
The LORD of Hosts, the mighty GOD,
   Th' eternal Prince of peace.

TRINITY SUNDAY.

PSALM LXVII.

1 *John* v. 7.

1 ASCRIBE immortal praise
   To GOD the FATHER's love,
For all our comforts here,
   And better hopes above:
He sent His own eternal SON,
To die for sins that man had done.

2 To GOD the SON belongs
      Immortal glory too,
   Who bought us with His blood
      From everlasting woe;
   And now He lives, and now He reigns,
   And sees the fruit of all his pains.

3 To GOD the SPIRIT's name
      Immortal worship give,
   Whose new-creating pow'r
      Makes the dead sinner live;
   His work completes the great design,
   And fills the soul with joy divine.

4 Almighty GOD to Thee
      Be endless honors done;
   The undivided THREE,
      And the mysterious ONE:
   Where reason fails with all her pow'rs,
   There faith prevails, and love adores.

2 Cor. xiii. 14.

1 BLEST be the FATHER and His love,
 To whose celestial source we owe,
Rivers of endless joys above,
 And rills of comfort here below!

2 Glory to Thee great SON of GOD!
 Forth fom Thy wounded body rolls
A precious stream of vital blood,
 Pardon and life for dying souls.

3 We give the sacred SPIRIT praise,
 Who in our hearts of sin and woe,
Makes living springs of grace arise,
 And into boundless glory flow.

4 Thus GOD the FATHER. GOD the SON,
 And GOD the SPIRIT we adore,
To whom be equal honors done,
 By all the Church, for evermore.

230

Rev. v. 13.

1 GLORY to GOD on high,
 The GOD of love and pow'r
Who made both earth and sky,
 Let all His works adore;
Praise to th': Eternal GOD be giv'n,
By all in earth, and all in heav'n.

2 Hail, all-sufficient LAMB,
 GOD, bless'd for evermore!

We glory in Thy name,
Thy fulness, love, and pow'r
Worthy art Thou, who once was slain,
Thro' endless years to live and reign.

3 O HOLY GHOST, to Thee,
   To Thee our hearts we raise!
   Accept our humble lay,
   And deign t' inspire our praise.
THEE TRIUNE GOD we trust to adore,
When heav'n and earth are known no more.

Rev. i. 5, 6.   P. M.

1 SING Hallelujah! praise the LORD!
   Sing with a cheerful voice:
  Exalt our GOD with one accord,
  And in His name rejoice;
  Ne'er cease to sing, thou ransom'd host,
  Praise FATHER, SON and HOLY GHOST,
  Until in realms of endless light
  Your praises shall unite

2 May we to all eternity
  There join the angelic lays;
  And sing in perfect harmony,
  To GOD our SAVIOUR'S praise;
  He hath redeem'd us by His blood,
  Hath made us kings and priests to GOD,
  FOR US, FOR US THE LAMB was slain;
  PRAISE YE THE LORD. AMEN.

232 & 233

The First Sunday after Trinity.

Psalm cxix. 1st. Metre cxxii.

Rev. iv. 8, &c.   C. M.

1 HAIL holy, holy, holy Lord!
    Thrice blessed Trinity!
By all Thy heav'nly hosts ador'd,
    E'er man began to be:
Worship'd by all the saints below,
    The God of truth and grace;
Thro' faith the great Three-One they know,
    And triumph in Thy praise.

2 The upper and the lower choir
    Shall soon be join'd in one,
And both triumphantly conspire
    To worship round Thy throne:
Angels and saints, when time shall end,
    Shall all Thy love display,
And in Thy glorious praises spend
    An everlasting day.

233   L. M.

1 FATHER of all above, below,
    Thy praise let ev'ry creature shew,
In Thee who live, and move and are,
    The Father's Everlasting Son,
Eternal Sharer of His throne,
    Let all in heav'n and earth declare.

2 Hail. Holy Ghost! alike ador'd,
    One with the Father and the Word,
The Lord of Life, the great I AM!
    Co-equal, Co-eternal Three,
Thy glorious Triune Deity
    Let all eternally proclaim.

Psalm i. xvi. lxxxiv.

234

The Second Sunday after Trinity.

Psalm cxix. 2nd. Metre lxiii.

234

Luke xiv. 16.   C. M.

1 ARISE, my soul, with joy obey
　　The mandate of thy Lord;
" All things are ready, come away,"
　　Thus speaks the sacred word.

2 In Christ, the Father reconcil'd
　　Invites our souls to come:
The penitent He calls His child,
　　And kindly welcomes home.

3 O then return unto the Lord,
　　The world and sin forsake;
See happiness in Christ restor'd,
　　And all His gifts partake.

4 O come, and with His children taste
　　The blessings of His love;
While hope attends the sweet repast
　　Of nobler joys above.

5 There, with united heart and voice,
　　Before th' eternal throne,
Ten thousand thousand souls rejoice
　　In extacies unknown.

6 And yet ten thousand thousand more,
　　Are welcome still to come:
Arise, my soul, the grace adore:
　　Approach, " there yet is room."

　　　Psalm lxxxvi. cxxxv. cxlv.

The Third Sunday after Trinity,

Psalm cxix. 3rd. Metre.

235

Micah. vii. 18.

1 GREAT God of wonders, all Thy ways
    Are matchless, God-like and divine;
But the fair glories of Thy grace
    More God-like and unrivall'd shine.
Who is a pard'ning God like Thee!
Or who has grace so rich and free?

2 Sins of such numbers to forgive,
    Guilty, offending worms to spare;
This is Thy grand prerogative,
    And none shall in the glory share.
Who is, &c.

3 Angels and men, resign your claim
    To pity, mercy, love and grace;
These glories crown Jehovah's name
    With an incomparable blaze.
Who is, &c.

4 In wonder lost, with trembling joy,
    We take the pardon of our God;
Pardon for sins of deepest dye,
    A Pardon bought with Jesu's blood.
Who is, &c.

5 O may this great, this matchless grace,
    This God-like miracle of love,
Fill the wide earth with grateful praise,
    And all th' angelic hosts above!
Who is a pard'ning God like Thee?
Or who has grace so rich and free?

    Psalm iv. lxxxix. xci.

The Fourth Sunday after Trinity.

Psalm cxix. 4th. Metre.

236

Rom. viii. 18.   L. M.

1 LORD! what are all our suff'rings here,
  May we but with Thy saints appear,
And see the glories of Thy face,
Reveal'd in truth and righteousness.

2 Expecting blessings at Thy gates.
For Thee the whole creation waits;
And full deliv'rance seeks from Thee,
Thy children's glorious liberty.

3 O gracious Saviour, and our God,
Array'd in majesty and blood,
Be thou our life! our souls in Thee
Possess their full felicity.

4 All our immortal hopes are laid,
In Thee our Surety and our Head,
Thy cross, nativity and throne,
Are full of glory yet unknown.

5 O may our joyful faith proclaim,
Life thro' Messiah's sacred name,
A word of Thine Almighty breath,
Disarms the sting and fears of death.

6 Here may my soul for ever lie,
Beneath the blessings of Thine eye;
'Tis heav'n on earth, 'tis heav'n above,
To see Thy face, to praise Thy love.

Psalm viii. xc. xcv.

THE FIFTH SUNDAY AFTER TRINITY.

PSALM CXIX. 5th. Metre.

337

Psalm cxvii. 12.   S. M.

1 MY Maker and my King,
 To Thee my all I owe;
Thy sov'reign bounty is the spring
 From whence my blessings flow.

2 Thou ever good and kind!
 A thousand reasons move,
A thousand obligations bind
 My heart to grateful love.

3 The creature of Thy hand,
 On Thee alone I live!
My GOD, Thy benefits demand
 More praise than I can give.

5 O! what can I impart,
 When all is Thine before!
Thy love demands a grateful heart;
 The gift, alas! how poor!

5 Shall I withhold Thy due?
 Shall I ungrateful prove?
LORD, form this wand'ring heart anew,
 And fill it with Thy love.

6 O let Thy grace inspire
 My soul with strength divine;
Let all my pow'rs to Thee aspire,
 And all my days be Thine.

   Psalm lxxxii. cxxxii. cxlix.

The Sixth Sunday after Trinity.

Psalm cxix. 6th. Metre.

238

Rom. vi. 9. New Version.   C. M.

1 CHRIST being rais'd by pow'r divine,
    And rescued from the grave,
Shall die no more, Death shall on Him
    No more dominion have.

2 For that He died, 'twas for our sins
    He once vouchsaf'd to die:
But that He lives, He lives to God,
    To all eternity.

3 If then ye risen are with Christ,
    Seek only how to get
The things that are above, where Christ
    At God's right hand is set.

4 So count yourselves as dead to sin,
    But graciously restor'd,
And made henceforth alive to God,
    Through Jesus Christ our Lord.

5 To Father, Son, and Holy Ghost.
    The God whom we adore.
Be glory, as it was, is now,
    And shall be evermore.

    Psalm xxviv. xcii. cxvii.

The Seventh Sunday after Trinity.

Psalm cxix. 7th. Metre.

239
Psalm. viii.   L. M. Old 112.

1 IMMORTAL King! thro' earth's wide frame
How great Thy honor, praise, and name!
Whose reign o'er distant worlds extends;
Whose glory heav'n's vast height transcends.
From infants Thou canst honor raise,
And form their lisping tongues to praise.

2 When, rapt in thought, with wakeful eye
I view the wonders of the sky,
Whose frame Thy fingers, o'er our head,
In rich magnificence have spread;
The moon and stars with lustre crown'd,
That nightly walk their destin'd round.

3 LORD! what is man, that in Thy care
His humble lot should find a share?
Or what the son of man, that Thou
Thus to his wants Thy ear should'st bow?
His rank awhile by Thy decree,
Th' angelic tribes beneath them see.

4 Subjected to his feet by Thee,
To him all nature bows the knee;
The beasts in him their lord behold—
The wat'ry tribes, the bleating fold.
Immortal King! through earth's wide frame
How great Thy honor, praise and name!

Psalm xxvii xciii, cxxi.

240

THE EIGHTH SUNDAY AFTER TRINITY.

PSALM CXIX. 8th. Metre. Old 104.

240

1 O Praise ye the LORD, Hosannas repeat,
His love to proclaim, together we meet;
O may our thanksgivings like incense arise,
Thro' JESUS a living and pure sacrifice!

2 Whilst angels abound in praise to the SON,
The heavens resound with what He hath done
Their voices we'll echo, and honor His name,
Exulting in JESUS, FOR EVER THE SAME.

3 How vast was that love that pitied our state,
And sent from above a SAVIOUR so great!
The FATHER'S rich treasure, O may we receive
'Tis love without measure to all who believe.

4 In JESUS'S face the Godhead appears.
With fulness of grace to banish our fears;
Redemption is finish'd: the work He hath done
Let all the creation shout praise to the SON.

5 LORD, what shall we give for mercy so great
Devoted we'll live Thy praise to repeat;
With soul and with body we'll honor Thy name,
And shout hallelujah to GOD and the LAMB.

Psalm i. lxxxiv. cl.

The Ninth Sunday after Trinity.

Psalm cxix. 9th. Metre. Old 148th.

241

Psalm cxxxii. 7. 9.

8   ARISE, O glorious King,
      Into Thy rest arise, [ascend the skies
  While saints their off'rings bring, and praise
      Arise, Thy holy Church to own,
      O make Thy truth and glory known.

2   Thy Priests, O LORD, 'array,
      With righteousness divine   [shine;
  Let them Thy truth display, and in Thy glory
      Let Thy whole Church, Thy chosen rest,
      Be with Thy smiles and presence blest.

3   O King of glory, come,
      And with Thy favor crown   [own;
  This temple as Thy dome, this people as Thy
      Beneath this roof, O deign to show,
      How GOD can dwell with men below.

4   Here may Thine ears attend
      Our interceding cries,   [skies:
  And grateful praise ascend, all fragrant to the
      Here may Thy word melodious sound,
      And spread celestial joys around.

5   Here may Thy future Sons
      And daughters sound Thy praise, [ing days
  And shine like polish'd stones, thro' long succeed-
      Here, LORD, display Thy sov'reign pow'r,
      While temples stand, and men adore,

Psalm xlii. xcv. cxxxvi.

THE TENTH SUNDAY AFTER TRINITY.

Psalm cxix. 10th. Metre.

242
L. M.

1 O For a bright inspiring ray,
  To animate our feeble strains,
From the bright realms of endless day
  The blissful realms where Jesus reigns!

2 There, low before His glorious throne,
  Adoring saints and angels fall;
And, with delightful worship, own
  His smile their bliss, their heav'n, their all.

3 Immortal glories crown His head,
  While tuneful hallelujahs rise:
And love, and joy, and triumph spread
  Through all the regions of the skies.

4 He smiles, and seraphs tune their songs
  To boundless rapture while they gaze:
Ten thousand thousand joyful tongues
  Resound His everlasting praise.

5 There all the ransom'd of the Lamb
  Shall join at last the heav'nly choir;
O may the joy inspiring theme
  Now warm our hearts with holy fire!

6 Blest Saviour, let Thy Spirit seal
  Our title to that blissful place;
'Till death removes this earthly veil,
  And glory crowns Thy saving grace.

Psalm xv. xlviii. xcvii. cxlvii.

243

The Eleventh Sunday after Trinity.

Psalm cxix. 11th. Metre.

243

1 *Cor.* xv. 3, 4.   L. M.

1 AWAKE a tune of lofty praise,
  To great JEHOVAH's equal SON!
 Awake, my voice, in heav'nly lays,
  Proclaim the wonders He hath done.

2 Sing how He left the world of light,
  And the bright robes He wore above
 How swift and joyful was His flight,
  On wings of everlasting love!

3 Deep in the shades of gloomy death
  Th' almighty captive Pris'ner lay:
 Th' almighty Captive left the earth,
  And rose to everlasting day.

4 Lift up your eyes, ye sons of light,
  Up to His throne of shining grace;
 See what immortal glories sit
  Round the sweet beauties of His face!

5 Amongst a thousand harps and songs,
  JESUS the GOD exalted reigns:
 His sacred name fills all their tongues,
  And echoes thro' the heav'nly plains.

Psalm xxii. lvii. cxlv. 2nd. part.

The Twelfth Sunday after Trinity.

Psalm cxix. 12th. Metre.

244

2 Cor. iii. 8. 9. L. M.

1 JEHOVAH reigns, His throne is high,
His robes are light and majesty!
His glory shines with beams so bright,
No mortal can sustain the sight.

2 His terrors keep the world in awe,
His justice guards His holy law;
But in His gospel shines His grace,
The glory of His righteousness.

3 Resplendent there His wisdom shines,
His truth displays His grand designs;
His pow'r is sov'reign to fulfil
The noblest counsel of His will.

4 His mercy, like a boundless sea,
Washes our load of guilt away;
While His own Son came down and died,
T' engage His justice on our side.

5 Each of His words demands my faith;
O may I rest on all He saith:
His truth inviolably keeps
The largest promise of His lips.

6 Descend, O glorious Lord, descend
To be my Father, and my Friend!
Then shall my songs with angels join,
And all the glory, Lord, be Thine.

Psalm xlvii. lxiii. cxlvi.

THE THIRTEENTH SUNDAY AFTER TRINITY.

Psalm cxix. 13th Metre.

245

Luke x. 37. L. M.

1 O What stupendous mercy shines
   Around the Majesty of heav'n!
 Jehovah deigns to call us sons,
   Our souls renew'd, our sins forgiv'n.

2 Go, imitate the grace divine,
   The grace that blazes like a sun:
 Hold forth your fair, tho' feeble light,
   Thro' all your lives let mercy run:

3 Upon your bounty's willing wings,
   Swift let the great salvation fly;
 The hungry feed, the naked clothe.
   To pain and sickness help apply;

4 Pity the weeping widow's woe,
   And be her counsellor and stay;
 Adopt the fatherless, and smooth
   To useful happy life the way.

5 Let age with want and weakness bow'd,
   Your bowels of compassion move;
 Let e'en your enemies be bless'd,
   Their hatred recompens'd with love.

6 When all is done, renounce your deeds,
   Renounce self-righteousness with scorn;
 Thus will you glorify your God,
   And thus the Christian name adorn.

Psalm lxv. lxxxiv. cxii.

The Fourteenth Sunday after Trinity.

Psalm cxix. 13th Metre.

246

L. M.

1 JESUS, how glorious is Thy name!
  The great JEHOVAH'S equal Thou!
O let me catch the immortal flame,
  With which angelic spirits glow!
As angels love Thee, I would love,
And imitate the blest above.

2 My PROPHET, Thou, my heav'nly Guide,
  Thy blest instructions I will hear;
The words that from Thy lips proceed,
  O how divinely great they are!
Thee, my great PROPHET would I love,
And imitate the blest above.

3 My great HIGH PRIEST, whose precious blood
  Did once atone upon the cross;
Who now dost intercede with GOD,
  And plead the friendless sinner's cause!
In Thee I trust; Thee would I love,
And imitate the blest above.

4 My KING supreme, to Thee I bow,
  A willing subject at Thy feet;
All other lords I disavow,
  And to Thy government submit;
My SAVIOUR KING, this heart would love,
And imitate the blest above.

Psalm xli. lxviii. xcviii. cxlviii.

247 & 248

THE FIFTEENTH SUNDAY AFTER TRINITY.

PSALM CXIX. 15th. Metre.

247   C. M.

1 MY hiding place, my refuge, tow'r,
    And shield art Thou, O LORD;
I firmly anchor all my hopes,
    On Thy unerring word.

2 Engrav'd as in eternal brass,
    The mighty promise shines;
Nor can the pow'rs of darkness rase
    Those everlasting lines.

3 The sacred word of grace is strong,
    As that which built the skies:
The voice, which rolls the stars along,
    Spake all the promises.

4 My hiding place, &c.

248

Matt. vi 32.   C. M.

1 FATHER, whate'er of earthly bliss
    Thy sov'reign will denies,
Accepted at Thy throne of grace,
    Let this petition rise;

2 " Give me a calm, a thankful heart,
    " From every murmur free;
" The blessings of Thy grace impart,
    " And make me live to Thee.

3 " Let the sweet hope that Thou art mine,
    " My life and death attend;
" Thy presence thro' my journey shine,
    " And crown my journey's end.

Psalm lxxvii. xciii. cxxi.

The Sixteenth Sunday after Trinity.

Psalm cxix. 16th Metre.

249

L. M.

1 GREAT God, this sacred day of Thine
  Demands our souls' collected powers;
  May we employ in work divine,
  These solemn, these devoted hours!
O may our souls adoring, own
The grace, which calls us to Thy throne.

2 Hence, ye vain cares and trifles, fly;
  Where God resides appear no more,
  Omniscient God! Thy piercing eye
  Can every secret thought explore!
O may Thy grace our hearts refine,
And fix our thoughts on things divine.

3 The word of life dispens'd to-day,
  Invites us to a heav'nly feast;
  May every ear the call obey,
  Be every heart a grateful guest!
O bid the humble sons of need
On soul-reviving bounties feed.

4 Thy Spirit's pow'rful aid impart!
  O may Thy word, with life divine,
  Engage the ear, and warm the heart;
  Then shall the day indeed be Thine!
Then shall our souls, adoring own
The grace, which calls us to Thy throne.

Psalm lxiii. c. cxxxviii.

THE SEVENTEENTH SUNDAY AFTER TRINITY.

Psalm cxix. 17th. Metre, Old 104th

250

1 O Praise ye the Lord, in triumph proclaim,
And publish abroad His wonderful name;
The name all victorious of Jesus extol;
His kingdom is glorious, and rules over all.

2 God ruleth on high, almighty to save;
And still He is nigh, His presence we have.
The great congregation His triumph shall sing,
Ascribing salvation to Jesus our King.

3 Salvation to God, who sits on the throne;
Let all cry aloud, and honor the Son;
Immanuel's praises the angels proclaim,
Fall down on their faces, and worship the Lamb.

4 Then let us adore, and give Him His right,
All glory and pow'r, and wisdom and might;
All honor and blessing, with angels above,
And thanks never ceasing, and infinite love.

Psalm. lxiii. ciii. cxlvii.

The Eighteenth Sunday after Trinity.

Psalm cxix. 18th. Metre.

251

Matt. xxii. 41, &c. L. M.

1 BY all the hosts of heav'n ador'd,
See David's Son and David's Lord,
Exalted high at God's right hand,
While angels bow at His command.

2 Jesus, the Lord, our souls adore,
A painful suff'rer now no more;
High on His Father's throne He reigns
O'er earth, and heav'n's extensive plains.

3 His race for ever is complete;
For ever undisturb'd His seat,
Myriads of angels round Him fly,
And sing His well-gain'd victory.

4 Yet, 'midst the honors of His throne,
He joys not for Himself alone!
His meanest servants share their part.
Share in that royal tender heart.

5 Raise, raise, my soul, thy raptur'd sight
With sacred wonder and delight.
Jesus the great forerunner see
Enter'd beyond the veil for thee!

6 His kingdom never more shall fail;
He holds the keys of death and hell;
'Till foes fall prostrate at His feet,
And His full triumph is complete.

Psalm ciii. cxxxii. cxlii.

The Nineteenth Sunday after Trinity.

Psalm cxix. 19th. Metre.

252

Matt. ix. 6.   L. M.

1. O Lord of glory, Prince of peace,
    Engage my grateful heart to Thee,
Thou Fount of grace and righteousness,
    Of life and joy, and liberty!
Thy sacred blood thro' earth and skies,
Mercy, free, boundless mercy cries!

2 By faith, I to this refuge flee;
    Here is my hope, my joy, my rest,
My Father reconcil'd I see,
    Mercy's inscrib'd upon His breast;
Away sad doubt, and anxious care,
Mercy is all that's written there.

3 Thy pow'r was sov'reign to forgive,
    On earth, as in the courts of heav'n:
Thy mercy bade the sinner live,
    "My Son, thy sins are all forgiv'n,"
Help me to soar to Thy abode,
To die to sin, and live to God.

4 Help me to run the Christian race,
    And all Thy marv'lous love proclaim;
To glorify the God of grace,
    And spread the honors of Thy name,
Till hosts of heav'n and earth combine,
And praise, eternal praise, be Thine.

Psalm civ. cx. civ.

253

THE TWENTIETH SUNDAY AFTER TRINITY.

PSALM CXIX. 20th Metre.

253

C. M.

1 THE LORD of SABBATH let us praise,
In concert with the blest;
Who, joyful, in harmonious lays
Employ an endless rest.

2 On this glad day a brighter scene
Of glory was display'd,
By GOD, the eternal WORD, than when
The universe was made.

3 Alone the dreadful race He ran;
The path of suff'ring trod:
He died and suffer'd as a man,
He rises as the GOD.

4 He rises, who our pardon bought
With grief and pain extreme;
'Twas great to speak the world from nought,
'Twas greater to redeem.

5 In psalms and hymns His love proclaim,
With melody of voice;
Present your off'rings in His name,
And in His truth rejoice.

6 A blest eternity we hope
With Him in heav'n to spend:
Where congregations ne'er break up,
And Sabbaths never end.

Psalm cv. cxvi. cxlviii.

THE TWENTY-FIRST SUNDAY AFTER TRINITY.

PSALM CXIX. 21st. Metre.

254

1 O That the LORD would guide my ways
   To keep His statutes still!
 O that my GOD would grant me grace
   To know and do His will.

2 O send Thy SPIRIT down to write
   Thy Law upon my heart!
 Nor let my tongue indulge deceit,
   Nor act a faithless part.

3 From vanity turn off my eyes,
   Let no corrupt design,
 Nor covetous desire arise
   Within this soul of mine.

4 Order my footsteps by Thy word,
   And make my heart sincere;
 Let sin have no dominion LORD,
   But keep my conscience clear.

5 My soul hath gone too far astray,
   My feet too often slip:
 Yet let me not forget Thy way,
   Restore Thy wand'ring sheep,

6 Make me to walk in Thy commands,
   Tis a delightful road;
 Nor let my head, or heart, or hands,
   Offend against my GOD.

Psalm xxxvix. c. 2nd Metre cvi.

The Twenty-second Sunday after Trinity

Psalm cxix. 22nd. Metre

255

Psalm cxxxiv. L. M.

1 THY presence gracious God, afford,
  Prepare us to receive Thy word;
  Now let Thy voice engage our ear,
  And faith be mixt with what we hear:
  Thus, Lord, Thy waiting servants bless,
  And crown Thy Gospel with success.

2 Distracting thoughts and cares remove,
  And fix our hearts and hopes above;
  With food divine may we be fed,
  And satisfied with living bread;
  Thus Lord, Thy waiting servants bless,
  And crown Thy Gospel with success.

3 To us Thy sacred word apply
  With sov'reign pow'r and energy:
  And may we, in Thy faith and fear
  Reduce to practice what we hear:
  Thus Lord, Thy waiting servants bless,
  And crown Thy Gospel with success.

4 Father, in us Thy Son reveal;
  Teach us to know and do Thy will:
  Thy saving pow'r and love display,
  And guide us to the realms of day:
  Thus Lord, Thy waiting servants bless,
  And crown Thy Gospel with success.

Psalm cxv. cvii. cxlvi.

THE TWENTY-THIRD SUNDAY AFTER TRINITY

PSALM CXXIV.

256

Phil. iii. 20, 21.   L. M.

1 ETERNAL LORD of truth and love,
    Thine holy influence succour brings;
O raise and fix our hearts above
    The reach of these inferior things.

2 O for a sight, a pleasing sight
    Of our almighty FATHER's throne!
There sits our SAVIOUR crown'd with light,
    Cloath'd in a body like our own.

3 Adoring saints around Him stand,
    And thrones and pow'rs before Him fall,
The GOD shines gracious thro' the man,
    And sheds sweet glories on them all.

4 Set our affections, LORD above,
    Our conversation be in heav'n;
There bliss resides, and perfect love,
    There shall eternal life be giv'n;

5 There shall these mould'ring forms revive,
    And like His glorious body rise;
And, fashion'd like to Him, shall live
    For ever perfect in the skies.

6 When shall the day, O LORD, appear,
    That saints shall mount to dwell above,
And in Thy presence worship there,
    And view Thy face, and sing Thy love.
    Psalm xci. cvii. cxlviii.

The Twenty-fourth Sunday after Trinity

Psalm CXXV.

Col. i. &c.   P. M.

1 HAIL, divine, eternal Spirit!
    Bless the sower and the seed:
Let each heart Thy grace inherit,
    Raise the weak, the hungry feed;
        From the gospel,
    Now supply Thy people's need.

2 O may all enjoy the blessing!
    Which Thy word's design'd to give;
O may all Thy love possessing,
    Joyfully the truth receive;
        And for ever,
    To Thy praise and glory live.

3 Thanks we give and adoration,
    For Thy gospel's joyful sound;
May the fruits of Thy salvation
    In our hearts and lives abound!
        May Thy presence
    With us evermore be found!

4 So, whene'er the signal's given,
    Us from earth to call away;
Borne on angel's wings to heaven,
    Glad the summons to obey,
        May we ever,
    Reign with Christ, in endless day.

Psalm cviii, cxi cxlix.

The Twenty-Fifth Sunday after Trinity.

Psalm CXXVII.

258

Jer. xxiii. 5. 6.   L. M.

1 BEHOLD the glorious day arise,
    Messiah comes His saints to bless,
Proclaim His mission thro' the skies,
    Jesus the Lord our righteousness.

2 Judah and Israel shall repeat
    His praises, and each other love;
Gentiles shall worship at His feet,
    His name adore, His mercy prove.

3 Zion rejoice, the days arrive,
    See nations round Thy altars bend:
Thy children from the dust revive,
    Gather'd from earth's remotest end.

4 From heav'n, from earth, loud songs of praise
    The mighty blessings shall proclaim:
Blessings that earth to glory raise:
    The purchase of the wounded Lamb.

5 Higher, still higher, swell the strain;
    Creation's voice the note prolong,
The Lord shall, ever, ever reign;
    Let hallelujahs crown the song.

Psalm xvi. 2nd part. xxi. 2nd part. lxxii. cx.

N. B. If there be more Sundays after Trinity, they may be supplied from those omitted after Epiphany, reserving the above Psalm for the last.

Saint Andrew's Day.

Psalm CXXIX.

259   (Old 104th.)

Rom. x. 9.

1. ALL glory to God, let angels proclaim,
And join with the church to honor His name
All praise to the Saviour, incarnate, who bled,
And mighty to ransom, arose from the dead.

2. O may we believe the truth of His word,
Enabled to call on the name of the Lord !
All they, who trust in him, His goodness shall
The Lord rich in mercy, in goodness&love[prove

3. How glorious the sound of tidings of peace !
The Gospel of Christ, proclaims our release ;
Let angels, archangels re-echo the theme,
Amen, Hallelujah to God and the Lamb.

4. Proclaim the glad sound of mercy and love,
Till all the redeem'd assembled above,
Renew'd by the Spirit and ransom'd by blood,
For ever inherit the kingdom of God.

Saint Thomas the Apostle.

Psalm CXXVIII.

260

John xx. 24.   P. M.

1 PEACE be to this Congregation,
  Peace to ev'ry soul therein;
Peace, the earnest of salvation,
  Peace, the fruit of pardon'd sin;
Peace, that speaks its heav'nly Giver,
  Peace, to sordid minds unknown,
Peace divine, that lasts for ever,
  Here erect Thy glorious throne!

2 Prince of Peace, be present near us
  Fix in all our hearts Thy home;
By Thy word of promise chear us,
  Let Thy sacred kingdom come:
Raise to heav'n our expectation,
  Give our favor'd souls to prove
Glorious and complete salvation,
  In the realms of bliss above.

3 May the grace of Christ, our Saviour,
  And the Father's boundless love,
With the Holy Spirit's favour,
  Rest upon us from above!
Thus may we abide in union
  With each other and the Lord;
And possess in sweet communion
  Joys, which earth cannot afford.

The Conversion of St. Paul.

Psalm CXXXVIII.

C. M.

1 HAIL, mighty Saviour, how divine
  Is Thy victorious sword!
Thy foes their weapons must resign.
  At Thy commanding word.

2 Gird on Thy sword, most mighty Prince,
  Thy sov'reign pow'r display;
Thy majesty, Thy grace evince,
  Till all Thy foes obey.

3 Let Gentile nations long proclaim
  The triumphs of Thy grace,
And chaunt the honors of Thy name
  In everlasting lays.

4 The vict'ries of Thy truth complete,
  Till all the faithful race
Shall round the throne of glory meet,
  To sing Thy conquering grace.

5 Thy Church on earth with truth inspire,
  Encrease with pow'r divine,
Till ev'ry heart to Thee aspire,
  And all the praise be Thine,

6 To Father, Son, and Holy Ghost,
  One God whom we adore,
Be glory, as it was, is now,
  And shall be evermore.

The Purification of St. Mary.

Psalm cxxxiv.*

262   C. M.

1 HIGH let us swell our tuneful notes,
    And join th' angelic throng,
For angels no such love have known,
    T' awake a cheerful song.

2 Good will to sinful men is shown,
    And peace on earth is giv'n;
For lo! th' incarnate Saviour comes
    With messages from heav'n.

3 Justice and grace, with sweet accord
    His rising beams adorn;
Let heav'n and earth in concert join,
    "To us a child is born."

4 Glory to God in highest strains,
    In highest worlds be paid;
His glory by our lips proclaim'd,
    And by our lives display'd.

5 O may we reach these blissful realms,
    Where Christ exalted reigns;
And learn of the celestial choir
    Their own immortal strains.

* From the Appendix to the New Version.

Saint Matthias.

Psalm CXL.

263   L. M.

Matt. ii. 25.   (Old 112th)

1 O God of wisdom, God of might,
   Great Ruler in the realms of light:
   Whose truths are hid from prudent eyes,
   But make the babe and suckling wise;
   In mercy help Thy servants, Lord,
   To hear and understand Thy word.

2 Reveal Thy scriptures to our mind;
   Here let us heav'nly treasures find;
   Do Thou those sacred leaves unfold,
   Let us Thy richest grace behold:
   O let Thy Spirit lead us forth,
   And teach us all its endless worth.

3 Direct us, lest we judge amiss,
   Lest error cloud the hidden bliss;
   Th' ingrafted word may we receive,
   And back to Thee the glory give:
   O make us know, O make us hear
   The glorious tidings treasur'd there.

4 In Thee alone the weary find
   Rest for the heavy laden mind;
   Teach us to bear, as in Thy sight,
   Thy easy yoke, Thy burden light;
   Grant us Thy peace, and make us blest
   With present and eternal rest.

THE ANNUNCIATION OF THE BLESSED VIRGIN.

PSALM CXXXI.

Vide MAGNIFICAT 160.

264

Luke. i. 31, &c.   P. M.

1 HAIL, Thou long expected JESUS,
    Born to set Thy people free!
From our fears and sins release us,
    Let us find our rest in Thee:
Israel's strength and consolation,
    Hope of all the saints Thou art,
Hail! desire of every nation,
    Joy of every faithful heart.

2 Born Thy people to deliver;
    Born a Child and yet a King;
Born to reign in us for ever,
    Now Thy gracious kingdom bring:
By Thine own eternal SPIRIT,
    Rule in all our hearts alone;
By Thine all-sufficient merit,
    Raise us to Thy glorious throne.

3 HOLY GHOST, who without measure
    Dwelt in JESUS CHRIST the LORD,
Shed Thy love, in thy good pleasure,
    Now in all our hearts abroad.
May we triumph in Thy favor,
    GOD of mercy, truth and love,
JESUS CHRIST our LORD and SAVIOR
    Lead us to Thy courts above.

Saint Mark's Day.

Psalm cxli.

265

Eph. iv. 7. L. M.

1 FATHER of mercies, in Thy house
Accept our homage and our vows,
While with a grateful heart we share
These pledges of our SAVIOUR's care.

2 The SAVIOUR, when to heav'n He rose,
In splendid triumph o'er His foes,
Dispens'd His gifts on men below,
And wide His royal bounties flow.

3 Hence sprung the *Apostles*' honor'd name
Sacred beyond heroic fame;
In lower forms to bless our eyes
Pastors from hence and *Teachers* rise.

4 So shall the bright succession run
Thro' the vast courses of the sun;
While unborn Churches, by their care,
Shall rise and flourish large and fair.

5 Thy presence, Lord, their hearts shall know
The spring, whence all these blessings flow;
Let priests and people shout Thy praise
Thro' the long round of endless days.

Matt. xxviii. 20.

St. Philip and St. James.

Psalm CXXXIII.

266

James i. 2, &c.   L. M.

1 PATIENCE! O what a grace divine!
    Sent from the God of pow'r and love!
That leans upon its Father's hand,
    And learns by trials to improve.

2 By patience we serenely bear
    The troubles of our mortal state,
And wait contented our discharge,
    Nor think our glory comes too late.

3 Tho' we in full sensation feel
    The weight, the wounds our God ordains,
We smile amid our heaviest woes;
    And triumph in our sharpest pains.

4 O for this grace to aid us on,
    And arm with fortitude the breast,
'Till life's tumultuous tempest o'er,
    We reach the shores of endless rest!

5 Faith into vision shall resign,
    Hope shall in full fruition die;
And patience in possession end
    In the bright worlds of bliss on high.

6 Blest is the man, who patient waits,
    Perfect thro' suff'ring, like his Lord,
He shall the crown of life receive,
    Promis'd in God's eternal word,

St. Barnabas, the Apostle.

PSALM CXLII.

John xv. 12.   C. M.

1 O Let Thy love our hearts constrain,
    Saviour once crucified!
What hast Thou done our souls to gain,
    Languish'd and groan'd and died!

2 Teach us each other, Lord, to love;
    And in our inward parts
Let kindness sweetly write her Law,
    Let love command our hearts.

3 Giver of concord, Prince of peace,
    Descended from above,
Write Thy commandment on our hearts,
    Inscribe Thy Law of love.

4 Produce in us th' effects of truth,
    Abundant fruits of grace;
The unity of Christian love,
    Th' endearing bond of peace.

5 Teach us to glorify Thy name,
    Redeem'd by sacred blood;
Be works of mercy our delight,
    Well pleasing to our God.

St. John Baptist's Day.

Psalm CXLIII.

268

Isaiah. xl. 1. C. M.

1 "COMFORT my people," saith our GOD,
   Proclaim the joyful word ;
Let the whole earth repeat the sound,
   Salvation from the LORD.

2 Behold your GOD, the LAMB of GOD,
   Who takes our sins away,
Who opens, thro' the realms of death,
   The path to endless day.

3 Let Zion's sons the truth make known,
   The righteousness divine ;
See grace and peace and sacred love
   In radiant glory shine.

4 Be ev'ry vale exalted high
   Sunk ev'y mountain low ;
The contrite and the humble souls
   Shall His salvation know.

5 The heathen realms, with Israel's land
   Shall join in sweet accord,
And all that's born of man shall see
   The glory of the LORD.

6 Behold the morning star arise,
   Diffusing heav'nly rays ;
Hail Light divine ! guide Thou our feet
   To everlasting days.

Vide 159.

Saint Peter's Day.

Psalm CXLIV.

Acts. xii. 7. L. M.

1 GREAT God, what hosts of Angels stand
In shining ranks, at Thy right hand!
Array'd in robes of splendid light,
They spread their wings for distant flight

2 Immortal fires, seraphic flames,
Who can recount their various names!
In strength and beauty they excel,
And round the throne of God they dwell.

3 Herod attempts, but all in vain,
To bind Saint PETER in his chain;
At God's command an angel speaks:
Light fills the goal! the fetter breaks.

4 Send, O my God, Thy angel down,
Point out the paths to me unknown;
Guide and direct my doubtful way,
Lead me to realms of endless day.

Saint James the Apostle

Psalm CXLVIII.

270
C. M.

1 NOT unto us—to Thee alone,
   O Lord, be glory giv'n.
Here let Thy praises be begun,
   And carried on in heav'n.

2 The hosts of spirits, now with Thee,
   Eternal anthems sing;
To imitate them here, lo! we
   Our hallelujahs bring.

3 Had we our tongues, like them inspir'd,
   Like theirs, our songs should rise,
Devoid of strife, nor ever tir'd
   With grateful sacrifice.

4 Till we the veil of flesh lay down,
   Accept our humble lays,
And bring us to Thy sacred throne,
   To give Thee nobler praise.

Saint Bartholomew the Apostle.

Psalm CXV.

Luke xxii. 28. P. M.

1 BEHOLD, the LAMB in glory stands,
Incircled with His radiant bands,
And join the angelic pow'rs:
For all that height of glorious bliss,
Our everlasting portion is,
And all that heav'n is ours.

2 Who suffer with their Master here,
Shall soon before His face appear,
And by His side sit down.
To patient faith the prize is sure,
And they, who to the end endure
The cross, shall wear the crown.

3 Thrice blessed bliss, inspiring hope!
It lifts the fainting spirits up!
It brings to life the dead;
All conflicts here shall then be past,
And all His saints ascend at last,
Triumphant with their Head.

4 Redemption's glorious mystery
They then with open face shall see;
The beatific sight
Shall fill the heav'nly courts with praise,
And wide diffuse the golden blaze
Of everlasting light!

SAINT MATTHEW THE APOSTLE.

PSALM CXVI.

2 Cor. iv. 4—6.   L. M.

1 MY GOD, assist me, while I raise
  An anthem of harmonious praise;
  My heart Thy wonders shall proclaim,
  And spread its banners in Thy name.

2 Behold the light unclouded shine;
  O glorious gospel, all divine!
  In CHRIST is life and bliss bestow'd,
  The perfect image of our GOD.

3 When gloomy shades the earth o'erspread,
  "Let there be light," th' Almighty said:
  The glorious Gospel light displays,
  Diffusing far celestial rays.

4 Condemn'd the race of sinners stood,
  And awful justice ask'd for blood;
  That welcome SAVIOUR from Thy throne
  Brought righteousness and pardon down.

5 Ye saints, assist our grateful tongues;
  Ye angels, warble back our songs;
  For love like this demands the praise
  Of heav'nly harps and endless days.

Saint Michael and all Angels.

Psalm CXIII.

273

St. Matt. xviii. 1.　　　　　　　C. M.

1 SEE Israel's gentle Shepherd stands,
　With all-engaging charms;
Hark how He calls the tender lambs,
　And folds them in His arms!

2 " Permit them to approach," He cries,
　Nor scorn their humble name;
For 'twas to bless such souls as these,
　The LORD of angels came.

3 We bring them, LORD, by fervent prayer,
　And yield them up to Thee;
Joyful that we ourselves are Thine,
　Thine let our offspring be!

4 Ye little flock, with pleasure hear,
　Ye children, seek His face;
And fly with transports to receive
　The blessings of His grace.

5 If orphans they are left behind,
　Thy guardian care we trust;
That care shall heal our bleeding hearts,
　If weeping o'er their dust.

274

SAINT LUKE THE EVANGELIST.

PSALM CXXXVII.

274

2 Tim. 4. 6.   C. M.

1 THE race is run, the warfare's o'er,
    The solemn hour is nigh,
When offer'd up to GOD, my soul
    Shall wing its flight on high.

2 With heav'nly weapons may I fight
    The battles of my LORD;
Finish my course, and keep the faith,
    Depending on His word.

3 GOD hath laid up for all His saints
    A crown that can not fade;
The righteous Judge, at that great day,
    Shall place it on their head.

4 The sov'reign King of grace decreed
    This prize His suff'rings won,
For all who love and long to see
    Th' appearance of His SON.

5 Save me from sin, prepare my soul,
    O LORD, for Thine abode;
That face to face I may behold
    My SAVIOUR and my GOD.

St. Simon and St. Jude.

Psalm CXL.

John xv. 17.   S. M.

1 LET saints each other love,
   Be mindful of His word,
And patient bear what He appoints,
   As servants of their Lord.

2 Thus all the saints of God,
   His messengers and seers,
The narrow path of suff'rings trod,
   And walked this vale of tears.

3 Through great afflictions past
   To better worlds above.
And more than conquer'd all at last,
   Through our Redeemer's love

4 Suff'rers like them, beneath,
   Through much distress and pain,
Through various conflicts, griefs and death,
   We trust with them to reign.

5 The Lord our glorious King,
   Shall wipe our tears away,
And call us up His praise to sing,
   In everlasting day.

ALL SAINTS' DAY.

PSALM CXLIX.

276

P. M.

1 HARK! eternal praise ascending,
    Round the throne the concert stands,
Cloath'd in robes of white, attending,
    Palms of triumph deck their hands.
Multitudes of ev'ry nation,
    Join to praise the SAVIOUR's name;
Hark! they shout aloud SALVATION
    To our GOD and to the LAMB.

2 Lo! all angels join their voices;
    Lo! they fall before the throne!
Now the choir of heav'n rejoices;
    Now the Church of CHRIST they own;
Glory, honor, adoration,
    Wisdom, pow'r and majesty,
Sounded thro' the wide creation,
    To our GOD for ever be.

3 Let us praise, and join the chorus
    Of the saints enthron'd on high!
Here they trusted Him before us,
    Now their praises fill the sky:
Lo! we praise Thee, gracious SAVIOUR,
    Wonder, love, and bless Thy name;
Pardon, LORD, our poor endeavour!
    Pity, for Thou know'st our frame.
        Vide 167.

Rev. v. 11. C. M.

BEHOLD, the glories of the LAMB,
  Amidst His FATHER's throne;
Prepare new anthems for His name.
  And make His honors known.

From ev'ry kindred, ev'ry tongue,
  Behold the favor'd race;
What distant lands and islands share
  The riches of His grace!

Hark! how they join their blissful songs,
  With angels round the throne;
Ten thousand, thousand are their tongues,
  But all their joys are one,

"Worthy the LAMB that died," they cry,
  "To be exalted thus:"
Worthy the LAMB, our lips reply,
  For He was slain for us.

JESUS is worthy to receive
  Honor and pow'r divine;
And blessings more then we can give,
  Be, LORD, for ever Thine.

The whole creation join in one,
  To bless the sacred name
Of Him that sits upon the throne,
  And to adore the LAMB.

O may I bear some humble part
  In that immortal song!
Wonder and joy shall tune my heart,
  And love command my tongue.

278

HOLY COMMUNION.

278
L. M.

1 MY God, and is Thy table spread,
    And doth Thy cup with love o'erflow?
Thither be all Thy children led,
    And let them all its sweetness know.

2 Hail, sacred feast which Jesus makes,
    Rich banquet of His flesh and blood!
Thrice happy he, who here partakes
    That sacred stream, that heav'nly food.

3 Why are its blessings all in vain
    Before unwilling hearts display'd!
Was not for you the Victim slain?
    Are you forbid the children's bread?

4 O! let Thy table honor'd be,
    And furnish'd well with joyful guests!
And may each soul salvation see,
    That here its sacred pledges tastes.

5 Let crowds approach, with hearts prepar'd,
    With hearts impress'd let all attend,
Nor, when we leave our Father's board.
    The pleasure or the profit end.

6 Praise God, from whom, &c.

* From the Appendix to the New Version.

Rev. v. 12.　　　　　　　　C. M.

THOU God, all glory honor, pow'r,
　Art worthy to receive;
Since all things by Thy pow'r were made,
　And by Thy bounty live.

And worthy is the Lamb, all pow'r,
　Honor and wealth to gain,
Glory and strength, who for our sins
　A sacrifice was slain.

All worthy Thou, who hast redeem'd.
　And ransom'd us to God,
From ev'ry nation, ev'ry coast,
　By Thy most precious blood.

Blessing and honor, glory, pow'r,
　By all in earth and heav'n,
To him that sits upon the throne,
　And to the Lamb be giv'n.

280

2 Cor. x. 16.　　　　　　　　S. M.

JESUS invites His saints
　To meet around His board;
Here the whole Church delights to hold
　Communion with her Lord.

For food He gives His flesh:
　He bids us drink His blood:
Amazing favor! matchless grace!
　Of our redeeming God.

＊ From the Appendix to the New Version

3 Let all our pow'rs be join'd,
 His glorious name to raise;
Pleasure and love fill ev'ry mind,
 And ev'ry voice be praise.

281
1 Cor. xi. 23, &c.   L. M.

1 'TWAS on that dark, that awful night,
 When pow'rs of earth and hell arose
Against the Son of God's delight,
 And friends betray'd Him to His foes.

2 Before the mournful scene began,
 He took the bread, and bless'd and brake:
What love thro' all His actions ran,
 What wond'rous words of grace He spake.

3 "This is my body broke for sin,
 "Receive and eat the living food,"
Then took the cup, and bless'd the wine!
 "This the new Cov'nant in my blood.

4 "Do this (He cried) 'till time shall end,
 "In mem'ry of your dying Friend:
"Meet at my table, and record
 "The love of your departed Lord."

5 Saviour, Thy feast we celebrate,
 We shew Thy death, we sing Thy name,
'Till Thou return'st, and we shall eat
 The marriage supper of the Lamb.

282   C. M.
Eph. ii. 12, 13.

1 AND are we now brought nigh to God,
 Who once at distance stood?

And to effect this glorious change,
  Did Jesus shed His blood?

2 O for a song of ardent praise,
  To bear our souls above!
What should allay our lively hope,
  Or damp our grateful love!

3 Draw us, O Lord, with quick'ning grace,
  And bring us yet more near;
Here may we see Thy glories shine,
  And taste Thy mercies here.

4 By grace divine, O may we rise,
  In such a scene as this
And join the chorus of the skies,
  The saints complete in bliss.

283   L. M.

1 LORD, while Thy suff'rings I survey,
  And faith enjoys a heav'nly ray,
These sacred symbols of Thy pain
Present anew the dreadful scene

2 For mortal crimes, a sacrifice,
The Lord of life and glory dies:
What love, what mercy, how divine,
Where justice, truth and pity shine!

3 'Twas with our griefs Messiah groan'd:
'Twas with our guilt His soul was tried!
Our punishment He took, He bore,
And sinners liv'd when Jesus died!

4 Awake each heart, arise each soul,
And join the blissful choirs above:
May nothing tune our future songs,
But heav'nly wisdom, heav'nly love.

284   L. M.
Old 112th.

1 O Bread of life! giv'n from above,
   Pledge of MESSIAH's dying love;
This myst'ry ev'ry thought exceeds;
For *us*, for *us*, the SAVIOUR bleeds!
Gaze, O my soul, Thy pardon see,
And weep and look at Calvary.

2 LORD JESUS CHRIST, Thou LAMB of GOD!
Who gav'st for us Thy flesh and blood,
Descend, and consecrate us Thine,
Fill all our hearts with love divine.
Thee may we praise, till life be o'er,
Then die in hope to praise Thee more.

285   L. M.
Old 112th.

1 O Glorious ordinance, divine,
   Which blessings to our souls conveys,
Impart, with hallow'd bread and wine,
   The strength'ning and refreshing grace;
Thou type of heav'n's eternal feast!
Thou pledge of everlasting rest!

2 O Thou, who reigns enthron'd above,
Who suffer'd once for us below,

Help us to celebrate Thy love,
   And thus Thy death and passion shew,
Till in the clouds our LORD we see,
And shout Thy praise eternally.

286

Old 112t

1 MYST'RY of grace! th' Immortal die
   Who can explore the vast design?
In vain the highest seraph tries
   To sound the depths of love divine.
The LAMB of GOD atonement made,
He the last ransom fully paid.

2 Angels, Archangels, join your praise,
   In this blest theme your songs employ,
Let saints on earth their anthems raise
   In endless symphonies of joy,
Till all the Church before the throne,
The debt immense of mercy own.

3 Then shall the triumph be complete,
   Then perfect love shall ever glow;
There lost in wonder at His feet,
   Our praise no interval shall know.
There all His acts of grace record;
There be *for ever* with the LORD.

BAPTISM OF INFANTS.

Mark x. 14.   C. M.

1 BORN to fulfil all righteousness,
    Commission'd to redeem;
Behold th' eternal Son of God,
    Baptiz'd in Jordan's stream.

2 Vouchsafe, O Lord, Thy heav'nly grace,
    The sacred rite we own;
Deign blest Immanuel to accept
    The off'ring at Thy throne.

3 The mystic water sanctify
    By Thy effective word,
And make the child belov'd by us,
    Beloved by the Lord.

4 Descend Thine ordinance to bless!
    Descend celestial Dove!
This earthly nature renovate,
    Inscribe Thy law of love!

5 The taint of inbred sin efface,
    Wash with a Saviour's blood,
And let maturer life attest
    The cov'nant made with God.

6 Under Thy banner may we fight;
    Constrain'd by truth and love
Confess our Saviour here below,
    Then shout His praise above.

BAPTISM OF ADULTS.

288

L. M.

1 GO, teach the nations, and Baptize,
 Aloud th' ascending SAVIOUR cries;
 His glad apostles took the word
 And round the nations preach'd the LORD.

2 LORD in Thy house, we seek Thy face,
 Now crown Thy ord'nance with Thy grace,
 Refresh our souls with truth divine,
 Let beams of heav'nly glory shine.

3 Eternal SPIRIT, Sacred DOVE,
 On this baptismal water move,
 And grant with energy divine,
 The inward grace to crown the sign.

4 Praise GOD from whom all blessings flow,
 Praise Him all creatures here below;
 Praise Him above, ye heav'nly host,
 Praise FATHER, SON, and HOLY GHOST!

CONFIRMATION.

289

Deut. xxvi. 16, 17. 1 *Chron.* xvi. 14, 15,

1 O Happy day, that fix'd my choice
   On Thee, my SAVIOUR, and my GOD!
Well may this glowing heart rejoice,
   And tell Thy goodness all abroad.

2 O happy bond, that seals my vows
   To Him, who merits all my love!
Let cheerful anthems fill His house,
   While to His sacred throne I move.

3 'Tis done; the great transaction's done!
   Deign gracious LORD, to make me Thine!
Help me, thro' grace, to follow on,
   Glad to confess Thy voice divine.

4 Here rest my oft divided heart,
   Fix'd on Thy GOD, Thy SAVIOUR rest!
Who with the world would grieve to part,
   When call'd on angels' food to feast?

5 High heav'n, that heard the solemn vow,
   That vow renew'd shall daily hear;
'Till in life's latest hour I bow,
   And bless in death a bond so dear.

6 Lord, in Thy holy Church encrease
  The gifts of wisdom, truth and peace;
  May all these solemn seasons see
  New sons and daughters born for Thee.

290

Gen. xviii. 17.   L. M.

1 FATHER of All, Thy care we bless,
  Which crowns our families with peace
  From Thee they spring, and by Thy hand,
  They have been, and are still sustain'd.

2 To God, most worthy to be prais'd,
  Be our domestic altars rais'd;
  Who, Lord of heav'n, scorns not to dwell
  With saints in their obscurest cell.

3 To Thee may each united house,
  Morning and night, present its vows;
  Our families and rising race
  Be taught Thy precepts, and Thy grace.

4 O may each future age proclaim
  The honors of Thy glorious name;
  While, pleas'd and thankful, we remove
  To join the family above.

FUNERAL HYMNS.

291
L. M.

1 BLEST are the dead, in Christ who slee
While o'er their mould'ring dust we wee
O faithful Saviour, Thou wilt come,
That dust to ransom from the tomb.

2 They rest from toil, the Spirit saith;
Their works of mercy, wrought in faith,
Shall find acceptance with their Lord,
And follow them with full reward.

3 Lord, when our spirits we resign,
Around us let Thy glory shine:
May we behold Thy blissful face,
Accepted thro' Thy righteousness.

4 This life's a dream, an empty show;
But that, to which the faithful go,
Hath joys substantial and sincere,
O may I wake and find me there.

5 O glorious hour! O blest abode!
Saints shall be near and like their God,
And flesh and sin no more controul
The sacred pleasures of the soul.

6 Their flesh shall slumber in the ground,
'Till the last trumpet's joyful sound:
Then burst the chains with sweet surprise,
And in their Saviour's image rise.

1 Thess. iv. 14.   S. M.

1 THE spirits of the just,
    Confin'd in bodies groan :
'Till death consigns the corpse to dust,
    And then the conflict's done.

2 JESUS, who died to save,
    The LAMB for sinners slain,
Perfum'd the chambers of the grave
    And made ev'n death our gain.

2 Why fear we then to trust
    The place where JESUS lay?
In quiet rests our brother's * dust,
    And thus it seems to say.

4 " Forbear my friends, to weep,
    " Since death has lost its sting;
" Those christians, that in JESUS sleep,
    "Our GOD will with Him bring."

5 This message then receive,
    And grief indulge no more ;
Be active here for GOD ; believe ;
    And wait the welcome hour.

* Or Sisters.

Psalm xxxix. 4. L. M.

1 OFT as the bell, with solemn toll,
 Speaks the departure of a soul,
Let each one ask himself, "Am I
Prepar'd, should I be call'd to die?"

2 Lord Jesus! help me now to flee,
And seek my hope alone in Thee;
Pardon my sins; Thy Spirit give,
And to Thy glory let me live.

3 Then when the solemn bell I hear,
If sav'd from sin, I need not fear;
Nor would the thought distressing be,
Perhaps it next may toll for me.

4 Rather, my spirit would rejoice,
And long, and wish, to hear Thy voice;
Glad when it bids me earth resign,
And rise to heav'n, by grace divine.

5 Prepare me, Lord, for thine abode;
My soul, prepare to meet Thy God,
Him serve on earth, then soar away,
To realms of everlasting day.

Vide Psalm xc.

PSALMS OF PRAYER AND PRAISE FOR PROTECTION AND VICTORY BY SEA AND LAND.

Psalm CVII. 2nd Metre. L. M.

294

Now may the God of pow'r and grace,
 Attend His people's humble cry!
Jehovah hears when Israel prays,
 And brings deliv'rance from on high.

2 The name of Jacob's God defends,
 Better than shields or brazen walls;
He from His sanctuary sends
 Succour and strength, when Zion calls.

3 Our God remembers all our sighs,
 His love exceeds our best deserts;
His love accepts the sacrifice
 Of humble groans and broken hearts.

4 In His salvation is our hope,
 And in the name of Israel's God;
Our troops shall lift their banners up,
 Our navies spread their flags abroad.

5 Some trust in horses train'd for war,
 And some of chariots make their boast;
Our surest expectations are
 From Thee the Lord of heav'nly hosts.

FOR A GENERAL FAST.

295

L. M.

1 WHILE o'er our guilty land, O Lord,
We view the terrors of Thy sword,
Before Thy throne of grace we fall,
And, prostrate, on thy mercy call.

2 Lord, help us to repent and mourn,
Turn us, O Lord, to Thee we turn;
O spare our land, in mercy spare
The Church Thy right hand planted here

3 Our King protect, our Councils guide,
Bid war's destructive rage subside;
Let Thy right hand our cause maintain,
And peace resume her gentle reign.

4 Our Fathers, Lord, in days of old,
Thy mighty works, exulting, told;
And may our nation, to the end,
Jehovah prove her God and Friend.

Vide Psalms of Prayer and Humiliation.

Psalm xlviii—li—xci—xciii—xcix—cxlvi—cxxi—cxxv—cxxx—cxlii—180—190—193,

296

FOR A DAY OF THANKSGIVING.

296

L. M.

1 MY God, my King, Thy various praise
Shall fill the remnant of my days,
Thy grace employ my humble tongue,
Till death and glory raise the song.

2 The wings of ev'ry hour shall bear
Some thankful tribute to Thine ear;
And ev'ry setting sun shall see
New works of duty done for Thee.

3 Thy truth and justice I'll proclaim;
Thy bounty flows an endless stream,
Thy mercy swift, Thine anger slow,
But dreadful to the stubborn foe.

4 Thy works with sov'reign glory shine,
And speak Thy Majesty divine;
Let *Britain* round her shores proclaim
The sound and honor of Thy name.

5 But who can speak Thy wond'rous deeds?
Thy greatness all our thoughts exceeds;
Vast and unsearchable Thy ways!
Vast and immortal be Thy praise!

Psalms of Praise lxxvi—cvii—cviii—cxxii—
cxxxv—cxxxviii—cxlvii—cxlviii-cxlvii 2nd.
metre.—cxlix—cl—173—175—183—250.

NOVEMBER the 5th.

PSALM XXXIV—LXXVI—CXXIV.

JANUARY the 30th.

PSALM XC—CXLII.—169—170.

MAY the 29th.

PSALM CXIII—CXVI—CXLVI.

THE KING'S ACCESSION.

1 Tim. ii. 1, 2.   Old 113th.

1 LORD, Thou hast bid Thy people pray,
For all who bear the sov'reign sway,
  And Thy vicegerents reign;
Rulers, and governors, and pow'rs;
And lo! we humbly pray for ours!
  Nor let us pray in vain.

2 O GOD, Thy chosen servant guard,
And ev'ry threat'ning danger ward
  From His anointed head;
Bid all His griefs and troubles cease,
Thro' paths of righteousness and peace
  Our King, propitious lead.

3 Cover His enemies with shame,
Abate their pride, defeat their aim,
  And make their counsels vain:
Grant Him a long illustrious line—
In Virtue's splendid list to shine,
  Through latest age to reign.

4 Upon Him show'r Thy blessings down,
Crown Him with grace, with glory crown,
  And everlasting joys;
While wealth, prosperity and peace,
Our Nation and our Churches bless,
  And praise THE LAND employs.

PUBLIC WORSHIP IN GENERAL.

298

EXCELLENCE OF THE BIBLE.

2 *Tim.* iii. 15, 16.   C. M.

Prefixed to the Old English Bible printed in 1607.

1 HERE is the spring where waters flow,
   To quench our heat of sin;
Here is the tree where truth doth grow,
   To lead our lives therein.

2 The tidings of salvation dear
   Come to our ears from hence,
The fortress of our faith is here,
   And shield of our defence.

3 Read not this book in any case
   But with a single eye;
Read not but first desire GOD's grace
   To understand thereby.—

4 Pray still in faith with this respect,
   To fructify therein:
That knowledge may have this effect,
   To mortify Thy sin.

5 Then happy thou in all thy life,
   What e'er to Thee befalls!
Yea, doubly happy shalt thou be,
   When GOD, by death, thee calls.

299 & 300

Luke ii. 12.   7, 7.

1 GLORY be to God on high.
  God, whose glory fills the sky;
Peace on earth and man forgiv'n,
Man, the well belov'd of heav'n.

2 Sov'reign FATHER, heav'nly King,
Thee we now presume to sing;
Glad Thine attributes confess,
Glorious all, and numberless.

3 Hail! by all Thy works ador'd!
Hail, the everlasting LORD!
Thee with thankful hearts we prove
Lord of pow'r, and God of love.

4 CHRIST, our LORD, and GOD we own,
CHRIST, the FATHER's only SON,
LAMB of GOD, for sinners slain,
SAVIOUR of offending man.

300

Isaiah vi. 2, 3.   7, 7.

1 LORD and GOD of heav'nly pow'rs.
                               Hallelujah!
Their's, and O benignly ours!
Glorious King, let earth proclaim,
Saints attempt to chaunt Thy name.

2 Bow Thine ear, in mercy bow,
Thou art LORD and only Thou!
JESUS, in Thy name we pray,
Take, O take our sins away!

3 Thee to laud, in songs divine,
 Angels and arch-angels join;
 We, with them, our voices raise,
 Echoing Thine eternal praise.

4 Holy, holy, holy LORD!
 Live, by heav'n and earth ador'd;
 Let Thy praises fill the sky,
 "Glory be to GOD on high."

301 7, 7.

1 MEET and right it is to sing
 Glory to our GOD and King;
 Meet in ev'ry time and place,
 To rehearse His solemn praise.

2 Join ye saints, the song around,
 Angels, help the chearful sound;
 Publish thro' the world abroad,
 Glory to th' eternal GOD.

3 Praises here to Thee we give,
 Gracious, Thou, our thanks receive
 Holy FATHER, sov'reign LORD,
 Ev'ry where be Thou ador'd;

4 Thro' the world's extent exclaim,
 Sing we praise to JESU's name:
 SAVIOUR, Thee we ever bless,
 Thee our LORD and GOD confess:

302 & 303

(104th Psa.)

1 O Praise ye the Lord, adore His great name,
   His worship extol, His honor proclaim,
Who for man's redemption, once offer'd His blood
All hail, holy Jesus! our Lord and our God!

2 Ye angels, on high, His goodness proclaim,
   From regions of bliss, in mercy He came;
For thousands of sinners the Lord bow'd His head
   For thousands of sinners, on Calv'ry He bled.

3 O praise ye the Lord, in glory on high!
   Let all the Church join the praise of the sky,
Immanuel's praise shall, while here, be our theme;
   Amen, Hallelujah, and worthy the Lamb.

303

Psalm xlv. 3.   P. M.

1 COME Thou incarnate Word,
   Gird on Thy mighty sword,
      Our pray'r attend:
   Come, and Thy people bless,
   And give Thy word success;
   Spirit of holiness,
      On us descend.

2 Come, holy Comforter,
   Thy sacred witness bear.
      In this glad hour:
   Thou, who almighty art,
   Now rule in ev'ry heart;
   And ne'er from us depart,
      Spirit of pow'r!

3 To the great ONE in THREE
  Eternal praises be,
    Hence evermore:
  His Triune Majesty
  May we in glory see,
  And to eternity,
    Love and adore!

304

Psalm lxxxiv. 1.　　　　S. M.

1 WELCOME, sweet day of rest,
    That saw the LORD arise:
  Welcome to this reviving breast,
    And these rejoicing eyes!

2 The King himself comes near,
    To bless His saints to day;
  Here may we meet, and see Him here,
    And love, and praise, and pray.

3 One day amidst the place,
    Where Thou, my GOD, hath been,
  Is better than ten thousand days
    Of vanity and sin.

4 O that my soul could stay
    In such a frame as this,
  And sing Thy praise, and soar away,
    To everlasting bliss.

305 & 306

P. M.

1 LORD of glory, and salvation,
  Reign ador'd by all creation,
    Men below and hosts above;
  Saints with praises, never ceasing,
  Worship, honor, glory, blessing,
    Chaunt the triumphs of Thy love.

2 Saints on earth, their off'rings bringing,
  Join the Church triumphant, singing,
    Ever be Thy name ador'd.
  Heav'n and earth unite their praises,
  One blest theme the chorus raises,
    HOLY, HOLY, HOLY LORD.

3 Praise eternal, praise ascending,
  Hallelujahs never ending,
    Through eternity be thine!
  Perfect with Thy saints in glory,
  Be our bliss to bow before Thee.
    And adore Thy LOVE DIVINE.

306

Old 148th.

Matt. xiii. 23. Rev. xxii. 20. 25.

1 ON what has now been sown,
    Thy blessing, LORD, bestow;
  The pow'r is Thine alone,
    To make it spring and grow;
  Do Thou the gracious harvest raise,
  And Thou alone shalt have the praise.

2 To Thee our wants are known,
    From Thee are all our pow'rs;

Accept what is Thy own,
And pardon what is ours;
Our praises, LORD, and pray'rs receive,
And to Thy word a blessing give.

3   Oh grant that each of us,
    Now met before Thee here,
    May meet together thus,
    When Thou and Thine appear!
And follow Thee, to heav'n our home,
E'en so, Amen, LORD JESUS, come.

DOXOLOGIES.

307

Old 113th

PRAISE GOD the LORD enthron'd on high;
    Praise GOD the SON, who deign'd to die,
And GOD THE HOLY GHOST adore.
Praise to th' Eternal Three be giv'n,
By all in earth, and all in heav'n,
    Both now, henceforth, for evermore.

308   S. M.

1 GIVE to the FATHER praise
    Give glory to the SON;
  And to the SPIRIT of His grace
    Be equal honors done.

2 To CHRIST th' anointed King,
    Be endless blessings giv'n;
  Let the whole earth His glory sing,
    And all the hosts of heav'n.

309

TO Father Son and Holy Ghost,
The God whom heav'n's triumphant host
And all His saints on earth adore,
Be glory, as in ages past,
As now it is, and so shall last,
When time itself shall be no more.

310

Old 113th altered.

TO Father Son and Holy Ghost
Give praise, ye saints, ye heav'nly host,
Through all eternity.
Let the whole Church her anthems bring,
Angels and saints Thy praises sing,
Jehovah sacred Three.

311   7, 7.

TO th' Eternal Three be giv'n,
Praise on earth, and praise in heav'n;
As it was in ages past
Is, and shall for ever last.

2 Sing we to our God above,
Praise eternal as His love:
Praise Him, all ye heav'nly host,
Father, Son, and Holy Ghost.

312

Old 112th.   L. M.

GLORY to God the Father give;
Glory ascribe to God the Son;
Glory to God the Spirit give;
Glory to the Great Three in One,
Angels and men the anthem raise,
A whole eternity of praise.

313

Old 148*th.*

PRAISE GOD, who reigns on high!
  Eternal anthems raise;
Praise Him who deign'd to die,
  The HOLY SPIRIT praise;
O praise Him, praise the sacred THREE,
In time and to eternity.

314

Old 104*th.*

BY angels in heav'n of every degree,
  And saints upon earth all praise be address'd
To GOD in Three Persons, One God ever blest;
  As it hath been, now is, and ever shall be.

315   P. M.
            8, 7.

SAINTS and angels, join'd in concert,
  Sing the praises of the LAMB;
While the blissful seats in heaven
  Sweetly echo with His name.
      Hallelujah! Hallelujah!
Saints on earth may sing the same.

316   L. M.

TO GOD the FATHER, GOD the SON
  And GOD the SPIRIT, Three in One,
Be honor, praise, and glory giv'n,
By all on earth, and all in heav'n.

317
L. M.

PRAISE God from whom all blessings flow.
　Praise Him all creatures here below;
Praise Him above, ye heav'nly host,
Praise Father Son and Holy Ghost.

318
C. M.

TO Father, Son, and Holy Ghost,
　One God, whom we adore;
Be glory, as it was, is now,
　And shall be evermore.

319
S. M.

1 THE Father we adore,
　　And everlasting Son,
The Spirit of His love and pow
　　The glorious Three in One.

2 At the creation's birth,
　　This song was sung on high,
Shall sound, thro' ev'ry age on earth,
　　And thro' eternity.

Public Worship—Vide Psalms xlviii.—lxv.
lxvii.—lxxxiv.—lxxxix.—xcii.—xcv.—xcix.
c.—civ.—cv.—cvi.—cviii.—cxxii.—cxxxii.
cxxxviii.—cxlviii.—cxlix.

157—158—187—223—225—226—231—240
244—255—257—258—259—260—261—262
265—268—270.

APPENDIX.

AFFLICTION.

The following are chiefly calculated for private devotion.

Psalm lxxvii.   C. M.

1 GOD moves in a mysterious way,
   His wonders to perform.
He plants His footsteps in the sea,
   And rides upon the storm.

2 Deep in unfathomable mines,
   Of never-failing skill
He treasures up His bright designs,
   And works His sov'reign will.

3 Ye fearful saints, fresh courage take!
   The clouds ye so much dread
Are big with mercy, and shall break
   With blessings on your head.

4 Judge not the LORD by feeble sense,
   But trust Him for His grace:
Behind a frowning providence
   He hides a smiling face.

5 His purposes will ripen fast,
   Unfolding ev'ry hour:
The bud may have a bitter taste,
   But sweet will be the flow'r.

6 Blind unbelief is sure to err,
   And scan His work in vain;
  God is His own Interpreter,
   And He will make it plain.

7 May I in confidence of faith,
   Then trust Thy grace divine,
  And credit what JEHOVAH saith,
   And know no will but Thine.

321   C. M.

1 IN ev'ry trouble sharp and strong,
   To GOD my spirit flies:
  My anchor-hold is firm in Him,
   When swelling billows rise.

2 His comforts bear my spirits up,
   I trust a faithful GOD,
  The sure foundation of my hope,
   Is in a SAVIOUR's blood.

3 Good when He gives, supremely good,
   Nor less, when He denies;
  Afflictions from His sov'reign hand,
   Are blessings in disguise.

4 Loud Hallelujahs sing, my soul,
   To thy REDEEMER's name;
  In joy, in sorrow, life and death,
   His love is still the same.

C. M.

SUBMISSIVE to Thy will, my GOD,
   I all to Thee resign,
And bow before thy chast'ning rod,
   I mourn, but not repine.

2 Why should my fearful heart complain,
   When wisdom, truth, and love
Direct the stroke, inflict the pain,
   And point to joys above?

3 Whate'er Thy providence denies,
   I calmly would resign!
For Thou art just, and wise, and good;
   O bend my will to Thine!

4 Whate'er Thy sacred will ordains,
   O give me strength to bear:
O let me know my FATHER reigns,
   And trust Thy tender care.

5 Why should I doubt His love at last,
   With anxious thoughts perplext?
Who sav'd me in my troubles past,
   Will save me in the next.

6 Will save, till at my latest hour,
   With more than conquest blest,
I soar beyond affliction's pow'r
   To my REDEEMER's breast.

7 To all Thy other favors add
   A heart to trust Thy word;
And death itself shall hear me sing
   While resting on the LORD.

323 & 324

Psalm lvii. 1.　　　　7. 7.

1 JESUS, SAVIOUR of my soul,
　　Let me to Thy mercy fly,
While the nearer waters roll,
　　While the tempest still is high:
Hide me, O my SAVIOUR, hide
　　'Till the storm of life is past;
Safe into the haven guide,
　　O receive my soul at last!

2 Other refuge have I none;
　　Hangs my helpless soul on Thee;
Leave, ah! leave me not alone,
　　Still support and comfort me;
All my trust on Thee is stay'd,
　　All my help from Thee I bring,
Cover my defenceless head
　　With the shadow of Thy wing.

3 Plenteous grace with Thee is found,
　　Grace to pardon all my sin;
Let the healing streams abound,
　　Make and keep me pure within;
Thou of life the fountain art,
　　Freely let me take of Thee;
May Thy peace console my heart,
　　Now, and to eternity!

324

Psalm lxxvii. 7, 8.　　　　L. M.

1 WHY sinks my weak desponding mind
　　Why heaves my heart the anxious sigh
Can sov'reign goodness be unkind,
　　Am I not safe if GOD is nigh?

2 He holds all nature in His hand;
 That gracious hand, by which I live
Does life, and time, and death command,
 And has immortal joys to give.

3 'Tis God supports this fainting frame,
 On Him alone my hopes recline;
The wond'rous glories of His name,
How wide they spread, how bright they shine!

4 Infinite wisdom! boundless power!
 Unchanging faithfulness and love!
Here let me trust, while I adore,
 Nor from my refuge e'er remove.

5 My God, Thy word of truth, indeed
 Is all my anxious heart can crave;
Thou present help in time of need,
 Almighty to relieve and save.

325
P. M.

1 GREAT God, unchangably the same,
 In all afflictive scenes, Thy name,
  Teach me, engrav'd, to view;
Teach me to see Thy hand divine,
Thy providence and promise join
  And own Thy record true.

2 To live to Thee be all my care;
 To trust Thee be my daily prayer;
  To honor Thee my aim.
My grand concern Thy grace to prove;
My lesson to discern Thy love,
  Thro' ev'ry change the same.

3 The end draws near,—when Thou, Most High,
Wilt condescend to justify
　Thy judgments now unknown.
Unfolded Providence will rise,
Glorious to our admiring eyes,
　When life's short race is run.

4 The veil withdrawn, Thy saints shall trace
The various leadings of Thy grace,
　And chaunt with seraph's love:
How glory, rich in heav'nly fruits,
Springs from affliction's bitter roots,
　In the bright world above.

326

Phil. iii. 20, 21.　　P. M. 8, 8.

1 IN a world of sin and sorrow,
　Compass'd round with many a care,
From eternity we borrow
　Hope, that can exclude despair;
Thee triumphant GOD and SAVIOUR!
　In the glass of faith we see,
O assist each faint endeavour;
　Raise, O LORD, our souls to Thee.

2 Place that awful scene before us,
　Of the last tremendous day;
When to life Thou shalt restore us,
　Ling'ring ages haste away!
Then this vile and sinful nature
　Incorruption shall put on;
Life-renewing, glorious SAVIOUR!
　Let Thy gracious will be done.

Vide Psalms xxii.—xxxiv—xxxix.—lxxi
xci.—ciii.—cvii.—cxxi.cxlvi.—170—171—
191;—271.—275.

330

Rev. xiv. 13.

1 REDEMPTION draweth nigh!
   My joyful lips shall sing
 Where is thy vict'ry now, O Grave?
   O Death, where is thy sting.

2 A voice from heav'n proclaims
   To all the pious dead!
 Blest is the memory of their names,
   Their grave a resting bed.

3 In CHRIST their LORD they die,
   Remov'd from sin and care;
 From suff'ring and from pain releas'd;
   And freed from ev'ry snare.

4 Far from this world of toil,
   They wait their Judge and LORD;
 Endued with everlasting life,
   Enrich'd with full reward.

Psalm xvi. 1, 2.

331

Luther's Hymn on the Judgment.

1 GREAT GOD, what do I see and hear!
   The end of things created!
 The Judge of mankind does appear,
   On clouds of glory seated.
 The trumpet sounds; the graves restore
 The dead, which they contain'd before;
   Prepare, my soul, to meet Him.

2 What millions do I see arise,
   To meet their Judge and SAVIOUR!
 What millions soar to yonder skies,
   Blest with eternal favor!
 Prepare us LORD, for Thy right hand,
 There may our souls accepted stand,
   And dwell with Thee for ever

Vide Psalm xcvii.—163—185.

332

The Glories of Heaven. C. M.

1 ARISE, O LORD, receive my heart,
   Inspire with praise my tongue,
And let the joys of heav'n impart
   Their influence to my song.

2 Sorrow, and pain, and ev'ry care,
   And discord there shall cease;
And perfect joy and love sincere
   Adorn the realms of peace.

3 The soul, from sin for ever free,
   Shall mourn its pow'r no more;
But, cloath'd in spotless purity,
   Redeeming love adore.

4 There on a throne, how dazzling bright!
   Th' exalted SAVIOUR shines,
And beams ineffable delight
   On all the heav'nly minds.

5 There shall the foll'wers of the LAMB
   Join in immortal songs,
And endless honors to His name
   Employ their tuneful tongues.

6 O tune our hearts to praise and love,
   Our feeble notes inspire;
'Till in Thy blissful courts above,
   We join th' angelic choir.

Vide Psalms lxxxiv,—167—220—231—242
256—271—276—277—279—286.

HYMNS FOR CHARITY SERMONS, AND FOR CHILDREN.

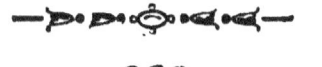

333 C. M.

1 BLESS'D is the man, whose heart expands
   At melting pity's call;
And the rich blessings of whose hands
   Like heav'nly manna fall!

2 Mercy descending from above,
   In softest accents pleads;
O may each tender bosom move,
   When mercy intercedes!

3 Great is the bliss, in wisdom's way
   To guide untutor'd youth,
And lead the mind that went astray,
   To virtue and to truth!

4 Let children your protection claim,
   And GOD will well approve
When infants learn to lisp His name,
   And their Creator love,

5 Delightful work, young souls to win,
   And guide the rising race,
From the deceitful paths of sin,
   To seek redeeming grace!

6 Almighty GOD, Thy influence shed,
   To aid this good design♣
The honors of Thy name be spread,
   And all the glory Thine.

334

1 COME, let our voices join,
  To sing a song of praise;
For favors so divine
  Our grateful notes we'll raise.
To GOD alone the praise belongs,
His love demands our noblest songs.

2 Now we are taught to read
  The Book of Life divine:
Where our REDEEMER's love
  Thro' all the pages shine.
To GOD alone the praise belongs,
His love demands our noblest songs.

3 Within this sacred house
  Our youthful feet are brought,
Where prayer and praise abound,
  And heav'nly truths are taught.
Great GOD accept our infant songs,
To Thee alone the praise belongs.

By the Congregation.

4 LORD, let this humble work
  Be crown'd with large success!
May thousands, yet unborn,
  This institution bless!
So shall Thy praise resound on high,
In time, and to eternity.

335   C. M.

1 FATHER of mercies! GOD of grace!
  Each perfect gift is Thine;
Through various channels flow the stream,
  The source is still divine.

336

2 Thy kindness call'd us into life,
　　And all the good we know ;
　Each present comfort, future hope,
　　Thy liberal hands bestow.

3 The friends, whose charity provides
　　This refuge, where to flee
　From want, from ignorance and vice,
　　Were raised up by Thee.

4 To Thee we owe the full supply,
　　Which by their hands is giv'n,
　To make us useful here below,
　　And train our souls for heav'n.

5 May health and peace attend them here,
　　And every joy above ;
　While we improve with grateful hearts,
　　The labour of their love.

336

1 HOLY, Holy, Holy Giver
　　Of all good, life and food;
　Reign ador'd for ever.

2 Leave me not, but ever love me;
　　Let Thy peace be my bliss,
　'Till Thou hence remove me.

3 Worship, honor, thanks and blessing,
　　One in Three, give we Thee,
　Never, never, ceasing.

(S-7)

1 GREAT JEHOVAH! GOD of glory!
 O let children lisp Thy name!
Humbly now we fall before Thee,
 Thy almighty grace our theme.
Hosts of seraphs join'd in chorus,
 Love divine proclaim on high:
Hear us, hear, O GOD most glorious,
 While the same blest theme we try.

2 Hail IMMANUEL! once incarnate,
 Bleeding, dying on the tree!
Little children Thou invitest,
 Without dread, to come to Thee:
At Thy word, behold us coming
 May we, LORD, Thy mercy prove;
Number us among Thy children,
 Thee to serve, and trust and love.

3 "May we live to know and fear Thee,
 Trust and love Thee all our days,
Then go dwell for ever near Thee,
 See Thy face, and sing Thy praise."
JESUS! GOD of consolation!
 Best of friends' in pity move;
Bless us, LORD, with Thy salvation,
 And accept our infant love.

N. B. If used as an Hymn for a Charity Sermon, instead of the four last lines, substitute the following.

 JESUS! GOD of consolation!
  Raise us friends, their pity move;
 Bless, O bless this congregation,
  And accept their works of love.

1 FATHER of all, whose tender love,
  Whose bounty all Thy creatures prove;
We feel Thy goodness, own Thy power,
Thy hand sustains us ev'ry hour.
FATHER! receive our hymn of praise,
Nor scorn the humble strains we raise.

2 Supported by Thy gracious care,
Thy blessings here we daily share;
Our infant minds, which else would stray,
Are early taught to know Thy way,
O may we ne'er forsake the road,
Which leads to heav'n, which leads to GOD.

3 O may Thy grace our hearts prepare,
Thy truth, Thy goodness to declare;
The kindness of our friends repay,
Guard them thro' life, to endless day;
For them our infant hearts we raise,
Impress'd with gratitude and praise.

To be sung by the Congregation.

4 Thou GOD of grace and mercy hear
This humble strain, this fervent prayer;
With all Thy choicest favors bless,
And own as Thine, this rising race;
Impress Thine image on their breast,
And guide them to eternal rest.

339.

HOLY, Holy, Holy LORD GOD of hosts:
  Heaven & earth are full of the majesty of
  Thy glory.
HALLELUJAH! AMEN.

FINIS.

AN INDEX.

A

All people that on earth do dwell — 100
All hail, Messiah, mighty Prince (2nd part) 18
All hail, victorious Lord (2d met.) — 110
Alas! and did my Saviour bleed — 202
All hail! triumphant Lord — 208
All glory to God, let angels proclaim — 259
And are we now brought nigh to God — 282
Arise, O King of grace, arise — 132
Arise, O Sun of righteousness — 178
Arise, my soul, with wonder see — 198
Arise, my soul, with joy obey — 234
Arise, O glorious King — 241
Arise, O Lord, reveal Thy face — 181
Arise, O Lord, revive my heart — 332
As pants the hart for cooling streams (2nd met.) 42
As pants the hart fatigued, distress'd — 42
At God's right-hand the Church is seen (2nd part) 45
Ascribe immortal praise — 228
Awake, my soul, and with the sun — 151
Awake, O sword, the Father cries — 199
Awake, my soul, and grateful sing — 219
Awake a tune of lofty praise — 243
Awhile remain'd the doubtful strife — 327
Awake, my soul, in sacred lays — 40
Awake my heart, with joy record — 45

B

Before Jehovah's awful throne — 100
Behold th' amazing sight — 203
Behold the Saviour of mankind — 204
Behold the glorious day arise — 258
Behold, the Lamb in glory stands — 271
Behold the glories of the Lamb — 277
Begin, my soul, th' exalted lay (2nd metre) — 148
Blest is the man whose heav'n-taught mind — 1
Bless God, my soul; thou, Lord, alone — 104
Bless God, ye servants that attend — 134

INDEX.

Bless'd angels, whilst we silent lie	153
Blesst be the God of Israel	159
Blest is the man, O blest of heav'n	32
Blest is the man whose heart	41
Blessed be the pow'r who gave us	200
Blest be the Father, and his love	229
Blest are the dead in Christ, who sleep	291
Blest is the man, whose heart expands	333
Born to fulfil all righteousness	287
Bring to the Lord, the mighty King	29
By all the hosts of heav'n ador'd	251
By angels in heav'n of ev'ry degree	314

C

CHRIST, the Lord, is ris'n to-day	207
Christ being rais'd by pow'r divine	238
Come, sound His praise abroad (2d metre)	95
Come, Holy Ghost, our souls inspire	222
Come, Holy Spirit, God of might	223
Come, Holy Ghost, Creator, come	224
Come, Holy Spirit, come	227
Comfort my people, saith your God	268
Come, Thou incarnate Word	308
Come let our voices join	334
Creator, Spirit, by whose aid	225

D

Day of judgment	185

E

ETERNAL Lord of truth and love	256
Eternal Source of ev'ry joy	173

F

FATHER of all, eternal mind	156
Father of all above, below	233
Father, whate'er of earthly bliss	248
Father of mercies, in Thy house	265
Father of all, Thy care we bless	290
Father of mercies, God of grace	325
Father of all, whose tender love	335
For Thee, O God, our constant praise	65
From all that dwell below the skies	117
Fret not thy anxious heart	37

INDEX

G

GIVE thanks to God, He reigns above — 107
Give to our God immortal praise — 136
Give to the Father praise — 308
Glory to Thee, my God, this night — 152
Glory to God on high, let earth and skies reply — 215
Glory to God on high, the God of love and pow'r — 230
Glory be to God on high — 299
Glory to God the Father give — 312
God of my life, look gently down (2nd met.) — 39
God is our refuge and defence — 46
Go teach the nations, and baptize — 288
God moves in a mysterious way — 320
God sees the good man's ways — 37
Great is the Lord our God (2nd metre) — 48
Great God, from Thy exhaustless store (2nd metre) 65
Great God, we own Thy sov'reign hand — 171
Great Judge of all, eternal King — 190
Great God of peace, and God of love — 206
Great God of wonders, all Thy ways — 235
Great God, this sacred day of Thine — 249
Great God, what hosts of angels stand — 269
Great God, what do I see and hear — 331
Great Jehovah, God of glory — 337
Great God, unchangeably the same — 325
Great is the Lord, his praise express — 48

H

HAPPY the man whose tender care (2nd metre) 41
Hail, Thou Source of ev'ry blessing — 177
Hark! the glad sound! the Saviour comes — 162
Hark! the herald angels sing — 166
Hark! the harmony of heaven — 167
Hail! Thou once despised Jesus — 195
Hark! the voice of love and mercy — 201
Hail! holy, holy, holy Lord — 232
Hail! divine, eternal Spirit — 257
Hail! mighty Saviour, how divine — 261
Hail! Thou long-expected Jesus — 264
Hark! eternal praise ascending — 276
Hear Thou my right, O Lord, attend — 17
Hearken, all mankind, give ear — 49
He that hath God his Guardian made — 91

INDEX.

He reigns, the Lord, the Saviour reigns
He dies! the Friend of sinners dies
Here is the spring where waters flow
High let us swell our tuneful notes
Holy wonder! heav'nly grace   (2d metre)
Holy Ghost, inspire our praises
Holy, holy, holy Giver
Holy, holy, holy Lord God of hosts
How long wilt Thou forget me, Lord
How are Thy servants bless'd, O Lord
How blest the sight! the joy how sweet

I

JEHOVAH reigns, His throne is high
   Jesus Chsist is ris'n to-day
Jesus shall reign where'er the sun
Jesus, how glorious is Thy name
Jesus invites His saints
Jesus, who once was dead
Jesus, Saviour of my soul
Immortal King, thro' earth's wide frame
In blessing Thee with thankful songs   (5th verse)
In thy distress the Lord attend
In Judah is Jehovah known
Infinite grace, Almighty love
In ev'ry trouble, sharp and strong
In a world of sin
In Thee, O Lord, I trust
In Thee, O Lord, I put my trust
Judge me, O God, and plead my cause
Judge me, O Lord, my trust art Thou

L

LET angels and archangels sing
   Let us praise, and join the chorus
Let saints each other love
Let joyful nations hail the day
Lift up your heads, eternal gates   (5th verse)
Lift up your eyes, to the heav'nly seats
Life now is past, the hour is come
Lord, when Thou didst ascend on high
Lord, for the mercies of the night
Lord, behold the hour is come
Lo! He comes with clouds descending

INDEX.

Lord, in the dust, before Thy throne	194
Lord, how are they increased, who rise	3
Lord, in Thy wrath rebuke me not	6
Lord, what is man? the pow'r of sin (2nd part)	8
Lord, what are all our sufferings here	236
Lord, while Thy suff'rings I survey	283
Lord, Thou hast bid Thy people pray	297
Lord of glory and salvation	305
Lord and God of heav'nly pow'rs	300

M

May the grace of Christ our Saviour	260
Meet and right it is to sing	301
Mighty God, while angels bless Thee	217
Mortals awake, with angels join	172
My God, my God, Messiah cried	22
My Shepherd is the Lord	23
My Shepherd is the living Lord (2nd metre)	23
My God, my everlasting hope	71
My Saviour, my Almighty friend (2nd part)	71
My soul, how lovely is the place	84
My soul inspir'd with sacred love	103
My soul repeat His praise (2nd metre)	103
My soul doth magnify the Lord	160
My song shall bless the Lord of all	165
My Helper, God, I bless His name	175
My blest Redeemer, and my God	180
My Maker and my King	237
My hiding place, my refuge, tow'r	247
My God, assist me, while I raise	272
My God, and is Thy table spread	278
Myst'ry of grace! th' Immortal dies	286
My God, my King, Thy various praise	296
My heart oppress'd with deep concern	36
My God, the transient life of man	39

N

Now may the God of pow'r and grace	294
Now from the altar of my heart	155
Not unto us, to Thee alone	270

O

O all ye people, anthems raise	47
O bread of life, giv'n from above	284

INDEX,

O come, loud anthems let us sing
O'er the gloomy hills of darkness
Oft as the bell with solemn toll
O for a bright inspsring ray
O God of truth and righteousness
O God, our help in days of old
O God, my gracious God, to Thee
O God, my God, my all Thou art   (2nd metre)
O God of hosts the mighty Lord
O God, our help in ages past
O God, my heart is fully bent
O God of wisdom, God of might
O glorious ordinance divine
O happy day, that fix'd my choice
O highly favor'd happy man   (2nd metre)
O let Thy love our hearts constrain
O Lord, our Lord, how great Thy name
O Lord, turn not Thy face away
O Lord of glory, Prince of peace
O Lord, rebuke me not in wrath
O Lord, my God, in Thee I trust
O Lord, arise and help Thy church
On what has now been sown
O praise the Lord with one consent
O praise the Lord, and thou, my soul
O praise ye the Lord, prepare your glad voice
O praise ye the Lord, prepare a new song
O praise the Lord, unite to praise
O praise ye the Lord, hosannas repeat
O praise ye the Lord, in triumph proclaim
O praise ye the Lord, adore his great name
O render thanks and bless the Lord
O render thanks to God above
O Thou, that hast redemption wrought
O Thou, in whom the Gentiles trust
O the delights, the heav'nly joy
O that the Lord would guide my way
Out of the depth of self-despair
Our Lord is risen from the dead
O what stupendous mercy shines

INDEX.

P

PATIENCE! O what a grace divine	266
Peace be to this congregation	260
Plead Thou my cause, O Lord, my God	35
Ponder my words, O Lord, give ear	5
Praise ye the Lord, 'tis good to raise	147
Praise ye the Lord, our God to praise	111
Praise ye the Lord, immortal choir	148
Praise ye the Lord, who reigns above	150
Praise God the Lord, enthron'd on high	307
Praise God, who reigns on high	313
Praise God, from whom all blessings flow	317
Preserve me, Lord; in Thee I trust	16
Preserve me, Lord, the Saviour cried	16
Prostrate, blest Saviour, at Thy feet	193

R

REDEMPTION draweth nigh	330
Rejoice ye righteous in the Lord	33
Rising from the promis'd nation	164

S

SAINTS and angels join'd in concert	315
See Israel's gentle Shepherd stands	273
Shew pity, Lord; O Lord, forgive	51
Sing to the Lord a noble song	216
Sing Hallelujah, praise the Lord	231
Sing to the Lord a new-made song	98
Submissive to Thy will, my God	322
Sweet is the work, my God and king	92
Sweet is the mem'ry of Thy grace (2nd part)	145

T

THE heav'ns declare the praise of God	19
The spacious firmament on high (2nd part)	19
The king shall in Thy strength rejoice	21
The Lord my pasture shall prepare	23
The God Jehovah reigns	99
The earth and all that dwell therein	24
There is a God, all Nature cries	14
Thou, Lord, my safety, Thou, my light	27
The mighty frame of glorious grace	196
The Lord is ris'n! he who came	210

INDEX.

The Lord of Sabbath let us praise	253
The joyful morn, my God is come	122
The heathen lands were forc'd to own	126
The spirits of the just	292
The Father we adore	319
The Lord, the mighty God comes down	50
The race is run, the warfare's o'er	274
Thee will I magnify, O Lord	30
Thee will I love, O Lord, my strength	18
Thee I will bless, my God and King	145
Thee, sov'reign God, our anthems praise	157
This is the day the Lord has made	118
This God is the God we adore	176
Tho' perfect eloquence adorn	188
Thou, my salvation, art, O Lord	27
Thou, Lord, by strictest search hast known	139
Thou, God, all glory, honor, pow'r	279
Thrice happy man, who fears the Lord	112
Through all the changing scenes of life (2nd part)	34
Thy mercy, Lord, to me extend (2d met.)	57
Thy mercies, Lord, shall be my song	89
Thy presence, gracious God, afford	255
To Christ the Lord, Jehovah spake	110
To bless Thy chosen race	67
To my complaints, O Lord, my God	86
To Thee, O Lord, I lift my soul	251
To thee, I cry, O Lord, my rock	28
To Zion's hill I lift my eyes	121
To God with mournful voice	142
To Father, Son, and Holy Ghost	309
To Father, Son, and Holy Ghost	310
To the Eternal Three be given	311
To God the Father, God the Son	316
To Father, Son, and Holy Ghost, one God whom	318
'Twas on that dark, that awful night	281

V

Vital spark of heav'nly flame	323

W

WELCOME, blest day, of days the best	187
Welcome, sweet day of rest	304
What shall I render to my God	116

INDEX.

Who in the Lord Jehovah trust	125
Who shall ascend and dwell	15
While saints above in perfect strains	186
Who hath our report believed	200
When I the holy grave survey	211
What shall we render unto Thee	214
When all Thy mercies, O my God	174
While o'er our guilty land, O Lord	295
Why do the nations furious rage	2
Why sinks my weak desponding mind	324
Why standest Thou far off, O Lord	10
With glory clad, with strength array'd	93
With all my pow'rs of heart and tongue	138
With heart and lips unfeign'd	184
With my whole heart, my God I'll praise	9
With ceaseless praise I'll bless the Lord	34
With joy we meditate the grace	191

Y

YE saints and servants of the Lord	113
Ye works of God, in him alone	158

The *MUSIC* adapted to the *Psalms*, *Hymns*, *Chants* and *Anthems* of this *Selection*, consisting of the principal old Church Melodies, and some modern Compositions, with the Harmonies properly arranged, may be had of the Pew-Openers at Bentinck Chapel, St. Mary-le-bone, or at Mr. *CAHUSAC's*, 37, Devonshire Street, Portland Place—Price 7s.

Persons taking of this, or other Works of the Author's, any number, not less than Fifty, may be supplied by Messrs. Watts and Bridgewater, 31, South-Molton Street, Oxford Street, at a discount of 25 per Cent.

www.ingramcontent.com/pod-product-compliance
Lightning Source LLC
Chambersburg PA
CBHW022117230426
43672CB00008B/1412